Networking Works!
The WetFeet Insider
Guide to Networking

2004 Edition

WetFeet ®

Helping you make smarter career decisions.

WetFeet Inc.

609 Mission Street

Suite 400

San Francisco, CA 94105

Phone: (415) 284-7900 or 1-800-926-4JOB

Fax: (415) 284-7910

E-mail: info@wetfeet.com

Website: www.wetfeet.com

Networking Works! The WetFeet Insider Guide to Networking

ISBN: 1-58207-370-8

Table of Contents

Networking at a Glance

The Basics

- **Everyone needs to network.** Half the people out there are already networking actively—so if you don't want to forfeit the advantage in the job market to them, you need to do likewise.

- **Networking doesn't have to be difficult.** There's no need to pour on the charm, or force a connection that isn't there. If you ask thoughtful questions, listen receptively, and respond openly, you're more likely to build solid bonds with your contacts.

- **Have no fear.** Everyone has to start somewhere, and the worst that can happen is that a contact would decline your invitation to coffee and you'd ask the next person you have in mind. Start with a modest aim: lunch or coffee with one new person a month.

- **Get active online.** Start posting on mailing lists and bulletin boards in your chosen industry and other areas of personal interest, and consider starting your own website to strike up conversation with those who share your interests.

- **People are not stepping stones.** If you're smarmy or dishonest in your interactions, you'll burn far more bridges than you build.

First Steps

- **Know your purpose.** Be true to your purpose with yourself and others, and you'll be surprised how people rally to help you realize your dreams.

- **Get geared up.** Standard-issue networking equipment includes a business card, thank you cards, a resume, work samples, and clean, appropriate business-casual attire.

- **Pursue hot prospects.** Start with a list of people with whom you've discovered overlapping interests or mutual friends. Then introduce yourself to the first person on your list with a mention of shared interests and common friends, and invite that person to coffee or lunch.

Making Connections with Ease

- **Networking is not interviewing.** Interviews are usually agonizing for everyone involved, so don't treat your lunch meeting as an interview. Just be yourself, avoid the hard sell, and do your best to make it an enjoyable, two-way conversation.

- **There's a time and place for everything.** Set your networking dates for sometime during the day at your contact's convenience, in a lunch or coffee venue that's casual, comfortable, fairly quiet and not likely to keep you waiting.

- **Small talk is a big deal.** Given what you know about your contact's interests and accomplishments from your background research, have a few specific questions and surefire conversation-starters in mind.

- **Follow-through is key.** Send a personal thank-you note the very next day, but don't stop there. Keep your contacts apprised of your career moves, and let your contacts know whenever you come across any lead, connection, or opportunity that might be of help or interest to them.

Advanced Networking

- **Don't stop networking when you have a job.** Maintaining a strong network can help you excel at your job, and keeps your options open in the job market.

- **Make a smooth switch.** Some diplomacy may be needed with your current employer to explore your career options, but you should let your interests be known in your circle and pursue them through volunteering, taking classes, online forums, and publishing.

- **As an entrepreneur, you don't have to go it alone.** Nor should you even try. Your best and most loyal clients, vendors, staff and supporters will probably come from your personal network.

WetFeet®

The Basics:
What You Need to Know

- Who Needs to Network?

- What's in It for You?

- The Old Boys' Club

- How Networking Works

- Working a Room, and Other Misconceptions

- The Fear Factor

- Your Network (It's Bigger than You Think)

- Internet-Working

- Gain Advantage without Taking Advantage

We cannot live only for ourselves. A thousand fibers connect us with our fellow men; and among those fibers, as sympathetic threads, our actions run as causes, and they come back to us as effects.

—Herman Melville

Remember those dot-to-dot pictures you did as a kid? Connecting those dots wasn't always so simple—so sometimes you asked other people for hints to get you started in the right direction, and sometimes they asked you. Networking is a lot like that. There might be someone out there who can point you towards the next dot along your life path, and you might be able to do the same for that person. But you'll never know, unless you network.

Don't let the name put you off—despite how it may sound, there's no ensnaring involved in effective networking, and it certainly shouldn't be tedious. Networking is sharing your insight and experience and inviting others to do the same. If you've ever referred a co-worker to your dentist or asked a friend where she got that great haircut, you've already got a head start (no pun intended). Your mission with this book, should you choose to accept it, is to take the very basic idea of information-sharing to the next level, to establish an ongoing, friendly exchange of ideas and expertise with an accomplished group of peers and fellow professionals. By the time you've worked your way through this book, you will have established an impressive network that will give you a chance to shine in your career, and put you in a position to help others shine too.

Who Needs to Network?

You've heard the adage a million times before: "It's not what you know, it's who you know." And the reason you've heard it so many times is because there's some truth in it. A single tangential personal connection can lead you to multiple opportunities for professional and personal growth, from job leads to lasting friendships. For some professions, networking is practically built into the job description. How do you think sales reps generate leads, journalists find sources, PR pros land stories, and HR managers find promising candidates? If you aspire to enter or advance in any of these fields, you'll need to be able to network like a pro.

Now here's another statement you may recognize: "I'm no good at networking." This, however, is not a time-honored truth, but a classic case of false modesty. You may not think you know how to network, but that's what you're doing every time you engage someone you don't know well in conversation and discover interests and ideas you have in common. Perhaps the best part of networking is that moment of stunned realization after you've hit it off with someone new, someone you actually hesitated to meet because introducing yourself seemed awkward or intimidating.

Everyone can and should network—and yes, this means you.

What's in It for You?

Still not sure what you stand to gain from networking? For starters, consider the following five basic benefits of networking.

Job Security

Having a strong network gives you staying power in several ways:

- It boosts your reputation as a team player, one of the most desirable attributes in businesses hit hard by the economic downturn.

- It gives you the inside scoop on what it takes to impress the powers that be as well as constructive advice on how to prove your worth.

- It increases the number of people who are likely to lobby for you when management is handing out pink slips.

As employee communication research shows,[1] the most important conversations in the workplace about layoffs often happen not in the boardroom, but over the water cooler—so don't become so consumed by your performance that you neglect the office coffee klatch entirely (see "Truth Be Told: Advance Warning about Layoffs"). This network may be able to give you advance warning about layoffs, glowing recommendations, and even tips about other opportunities outside the organization. But don't forget about your network beyond your office door, either. Technology has been particularly hard hit in the past few years, and *Computerworld* senior columnist Frank Hayes recommends broad networking as one of the best ways to avoid the axe: "Join a users group or a professional society, and go to the meetings," he says. "Do favors for people who are looking for jobs."[2]

[1]Nancy Welch, Mark Goldstein. *Communicating Change: Ideas from Contemporary Research.* IABC Research Foundation, 2000.
[2]Frank Hayes. "Put Your Fear to Work." *Computerworld.* May 31, 2002.

Truth Be Told: Advance Warning about Layoffs

This networking timeline shows how layoffs worked at one struggling company:

One month before layoffs   The smokers in the office noticed the CEO had started chain-smoking, and the CEO finally confessed that pink slips were on their way.

Two weeks before layoffs   Word of the layoffs trickled down to friends and people who took coffee breaks with the smokers.

The day of layoffs Employees who didn't fraternize with their co-workers were shocked and dismayed to hear the news. Everyone else was able to take it in stride, with their resumes already in circulation.

Better Opportunities

Some of the most desirable job opportunities are those you'll never hear about unless you have a network that gives you the inside scoop. Especially when the job market is tight, many companies are reluctant to post attractive managerial job listings for fear of being deluged with hundreds of responses, many from unqualified candidates. Instead, they ask employees and colleagues to circulate the word, either verbally or via e-mail, among their colleagues and friends to find qualified candidates. If no prime candidates emerge, the job might be circulated to a slightly broader circle, through professional, alumni, and trade association e-mail groups and publications. If and when the job is posted on online job boards or in the newspaper, it's often just a formality—the candidates who emerge from personal or professional networks usually have the edge on the competition.

The more attractive the job, the less likely you are to hear about it through the official job-search channels. At the risk of stating the obvious, when a world-renowned rock band wants to find a new lead singer or the American embassy in Paris is looking for a new ambassador, they don't start by putting an ad in the paper. (Imagine the replies they'd get!) Instead, they put out feelers in their professional and social circles to find out who is talented, credentialed and available. (You might recall that the movie *Rock Star* is based on just such a story, when heavy metal megaband Judas Priest got the tip about a small-time impersonator who became their new lead singer.) The odds are, a famous rock band will hire someone who comes personally recommended by trusted insiders—and the rest of us will probably become aware of the job opening only when the new hire is announced. On the off chance they do post the listing in some obscure online discussion group or trade publication, you'll increase your chances of coming across that ad if a subscriber in your social or professional network notices it, thinks of you, and forwards the posting to you.

Less Stress

According to recent neuroendocrinology research,[1] people with strong social support networks are less susceptible to the unexpected and not as stressed out by setbacks. Your network gives you much-needed perspective and support in tough times and ample opportunities for stress-free good times, too. Think about how you scored those free tickets to that film festival you so enjoyed or wound up tagging along to that barbecue where you met your future boss— probably someone in your social circle told you about it or extended an invitation. Broaden your circle just a little, and there will be more invitations and newfound friends where those came from.

[1]Bruce McEwen, Ph.D. *The End of Stress as We Know It.* 2002.

Positive Reinforcement

We all want a chance to stretch and see what we're capable of, but it can be scary to take on challenging new assignments. Everyone experiences moments of doubt about their ability to realize ambitions and live up to expectations—but people who have a personal network have mentors and friends they can turn to for reassurance and constructive advice. The greater your goals, the greater the support network you'll need to keep on track to achieve them. Ever notice how Academy Award winners tend to thank scores of people and gush, "I couldn't have done it without you all"? Well, they aren't *all* faking it. No matter how talented you may be, your support network can make all the difference between an abandoned attempt and an award-winning success.

Stiff Competition

If the previous four reasons haven't convinced you to network, this one should do the trick. According to a survey initiated by The Creative Group, 48 percent of survey respondents are networking more than they were three years ago, with 21 percent reporting they are doing "significantly more" networking now.[1] That means you need to network if you aspire to even make it into the 49th percentile in the applicant pool, let alone compete for more sought-after jobs. Are you willing to forfeit your dream job and your family's prospects to someone who might be less qualified, less talented, less committed, and less in need of a break, all over a matter of what amounts to a few perfectly pleasant lunches? Didn't think so. Read on!

[1] The Creative Group press release. April 16, 2003.

The Old Boys' Club

Every one of us needs to network, but some of us have to work harder at it than others.

Fact is, only an elite few among us are born into the powerful family networks that continue to dominate business around the world.[2] In the job market, these contenders enjoy substantial educational, economic, social, and political advantage—not to mention that doors tend to open a lot faster when you have the name Bush, Vanderbilt, Kennedy, or Rockefeller on your calling card. If you don't happen to belong to a family whose name regularly appears in the society pages of *Vanity Fair*, you will have to make a name for yourself to get your foot in the door—and that means networking at least twice as much as the established members of the Old Boys' Club.

But there's a twist: Even the Old Boys' Club is no match for an active, developing network. A lucky few might manage to land a lucrative, important position through that elusive combination of dumb luck and powerful parentage, but no one should expect to stay there long without support. Family businesses are not impervious to competition—in fact, less than 15 percent of family firms survive under family control after the third generation.[1]

So don't give up your dreams of a decent living and a fair shot at success in the business world if it so happens that you're not old, or a boy, or a member of some exclusive club. There are plenty of alternative networks you can opt into that don't exclude people on the basis of parentage or personal finances. Look into professional, alumni, and trade associations, and sign up for mail groups for people who share your interests, enthusiasms, or hobbies. If you're

[1] *Knowledge at Wharton Newsletter.* University of Pennsylvania. August 27, 2003.

unemployed, you might consider joining a job-hunting club or support group to keep your options open and your spirits up as you look for work. If you don't find an organization, website, or discussion group that speaks to your specific interests, background, or goals, don't twiddle your thumbs waiting for one to spring up—start your own.

The odds are that you are not the only woman or person of your cultural background or sexual orientation in your field, of course, which means there are probably women's professional organizations, religious and cultural organizations, gay/lesbian/bisexual/transgender groups, and minority business alliances where you can find and exchange promising ideas, practical advice, and vital support. Many of these organizations offer a range of professional and career services, such as job boards and mentoring programs or help with business plans and small business loan applications.

But just because many of these associations and organizations are nonprofits, don't expect them to give you a free ride. Some organizations may charge a nominal fee for networking mixers or online job-hunting services and ask you to return the favor down the line by mentoring a newbie to your field. These "fee-for-service" offerings and volunteer commitments are increasingly important for nonprofits as they struggle to stay afloat in these days of limited government funding. And as with any networking effort, the people who gain the most are typically those who give the most. Volunteers and people who actively contribute their insights to online discussion groups tend to connect with more people than those who only occasionally attend functions or lurk online. So don't go to nonprofit and volunteer-driven organizations hat in hand—be generous with your time and insights, and be sure to give as much as you get.

As you tap these alternative networks, you'll build your own network one person at a time—and soon enough, you'll have the reputation and support you need to give the Old Boys' Club a run for its money. Rise to the challenge, lift your network up with you when you make it, and show the world that nice guys and gals don't always finish last.

How Networking Works

Each friend represents a world in us, a world possibly not born until they arrive, and it is only by this meeting that a new world is born.

—*Anaïs Nin*

Networking is not as complicated as it sounds. You meet someone with whom you share interests, you chat over lunch or coffee, you explore common interests, and you stay in touch. Points of personal connection may not always be immediately obvious, especially in the workplace, so you'll need to pay careful attention when other people are talking to uncover a common bond. Even with your best efforts, this may not always be possible—when you start inviting people you meet for lunch or coffee, you should expect that some of your meetings will be relatively uneventful and uninspiring. But when you do find a point of meaningful connection, you'll suddenly find that you and your contact are sharing something much more profound than lunch—and you'll realize that all those other meetings were a necessary warm-up to get to this one.

This personal connection is its own reward and can lead to a terrific friendship—but it can also have career benefits. Will you get hired on the spot? Almost never; but the benefits of networking are potentially far greater than a single job. A single promising contact could lead to not just one, but multiple job leads over the months and years to come. More important, networking can encourage you to pursue career aspirations you never dreamed were possible and change the entire course of your career for the better.

Paint Me a Picture

How does this work in actual practice, you ask?

Well, let's say that you're bored with your job writing corporate communications and are considering going into product marketing. So you start running Web searches and reading online trade publications on the subject, get up the courage to ask some questions about the field in an online marketing association forum, ask a few friends if they know any marketers you can talk to, and mention your interest to those in your alumni association. Eventually, you're introduced to someone who's in food product marketing at an alumni gathering. You exchange business cards, and the next day you follow up by inviting that person to lunch, where you discover that you both studied abroad in China as undergraduates. A lively conversation about Chinese poetry and cuisine ensues, and you part on friendly terms. Afterward, you send a thank-you note for the meeting, you have a friendly e-mail exchange, and you stay in touch off and on. You meet up once at a poetry reading, and you drop your contact an e-mail when you hear that a visiting chef from Shanghai is giving a demonstration.

What does this all have to do with your career? Not much—yet.

Then, a few weeks or months after your initial lunch, you get an e-mail:
It's your contact. There's a rumor going around her office that a marketing position
is about to be vacated, and they need someone fluent in Mandarin who can pick
up the overseas suppliers' end of the business quickly. Officially, you're not
supposed to be having this conversation, but she trusts you to be discreet.
They'd have to conduct an official search process—but rather than losing
momentum on their projects with a protracted search, they'd rather hire a
promising candidate soon on an interim-to-permanent basis. She remembers
you once asked her an insightful question about supply-chain management in
your discussions about marketing, and she wonders if this might be a niche that
would interest you. You could try it out for six months, she says, to see whether
it's a good fit.

Three months later: Thanks to inside tips from your contact, you're already
impressing the powers that be in your interim role, and you're in prime position
to negotiate an excellent salary should you decide to accept a permanent position.

Four months later: It's a friend of your contact, who mentioned that you
might be able to provide some tips on dining in the area where you lived in
China. You meet for lunch and discover your new contact is a lifestyle editor at
your favorite local magazine who's headed to China to do research for a travel
article on regional cuisines. After some discussion about the relative merits of
eel and catfish, the editor confesses she's far too pressed for time right now to
do the in-depth research this article clearly deserves. Clearly you're well versed
in the subject already—is there any chance you might consider contributing
some research for the feature? It would pay very little, but you'd get a "with
reporting by" credit in the magazine.

Six months later: When a regular contributor backs out on the job at the last
minute, the editor calls you up to see if you might be free this weekend to write
a short restaurant review of a new Cantonese restaurant, this time with your

own byline. If it goes well, maybe she could send some more reviews your way so she doesn't always have to rely on that flaky writer. The pay is peanuts, but this could be the start of the career transition you secretly always dreamed about: from the anonymous writer of Web content about employee health benefits, to celebrated restaurant reviewer.

Eight months later: It's a friend of a friend of your contact, who mentioned your interest in cooking and skills with writing promotional copy. This person is a chef who started a Chinese cooking show on cable access just for fun and is now developing a following, so he could use some advice about pulling together some promotional materials to pitch the show to a local PBS station. You go out for lunch and hit it off—and you offer some promotional suggestions and program development ideas your lunch partner thinks are genius. Would you be willing to look at a script sometime, to see if you might have any suggestions for touching it up?

One year later: Your Saturday morning hobby of editing the cable-access food show script has turned into an occasional freelance script-writer's gig for the home and garden segment of a local TV news broadcast, where your chef friend is now the regular food expert. Your company has granted your request for a part-time schedule, so you are able to pursue your budding broadcast career without losing the stability of a regular paycheck.

If any one of these career developments sound attractive, consider this: Over the course of a few years, that one initial promising contact could lead to not one, but all three of the career options described above. Then those may lead to other opportunities, which lead to others, and so on. In this way, networking can increase the opportunities available to you exponentially.

This is a dream scenario, of course, and most networking contacts will not yield this range of opportunities. And, likewise, most people do not network effectively

or often enough to take advantage of the multitude of possibilities a single initial contact may yield. You may have to go out for coffee with near-complete strangers ten, twenty, fifty, or even a hundred times before you get to that one person who you really hit it off with.

But this scenario does illustrate the domino-like nature of effective networking. Some important lessons can be gleaned from this scenario:

1. **You often won't be able to anticipate how a contact may help you.** Some contacts that seem particularly well positioned to help you may in fact provide no assistance at all, whereas others who have no obvious connections of interest to you may in time prove to be of immeasurable value.

2. **The most effective networking is always reciprocal over time.** Just as you stand to gain a lot, you also have a lot to offer. Whether you choose to think of it as karma or a potlatch, the idea is the same—it's an activity that eventually benefits most or all involved parties. And, if it doesn't, it's unlikely that many parties will remain involved.

Keeping It Real

If you keep up the networking, you will find that it's well worth your while as well as a perfectly pleasant way to get to know people besides. At its easiest and most intuitive, networking can be a matter of pursuing your passions actively and getting to know the people who share those interests—whether that's acupuncture, soccer, or knitting. If all of this sounds too good to be true, consider these real-life examples:

Coffee talk can win you a loyal clientele. A graphic designer studying traditional Chinese medicine in her spare time found her first acupuncture clients by offering suggestions over coffee to coworkers with aches and pains. These

coworkers referred her to other people, and she is now a partner in a holistic health care practice with hundreds of steady clients.

A Sunday pick-up game can yield hidden opportunities. Editors from a notable travel guide company organize a weekly soccer game, where fellow players hear about travel writing opportunities that are never announced to the general public. The readership of each guide during its life span is estimated at 5,000 to 10,000 readers.

Pursuing your hobbies can introduce you to influential contacts. A weekly "stitch-n-bitch" knitting session in one company's lunchroom has led to friendships and mutually supportive workplace alliances, plus great new product ideas. One of the founding members of this knitting group now runs the most lucrative product division, reaching some 75,000 households annually.

The Right Stuff

One problem is, the impact networking has on your career is usually so gradual and cumulative that you may not notice it at all at first. Many people fail to appreciate this, and when they don't get immediate career breakthroughs from networking, they tend to assume they're simply not cut out for networking. On the contrary: Networking doesn't require a specific personality type, but rather three key behaviors, all of which anyone can pick up with practice and may already come naturally to you.

Patience. Try applying some of the persistence and resilience you've gained from dating to networking. Keep in mind how many dates most people go on before they find a soul mate, and remember: Even the dullest chat with a contact over coffee is a lot less agonizing than a bad blind date. And if you don't hit it off with the people you meet at first, don't let it keep you up at night. Could be you

were doing fine, but the chemistry was slightly off. Life is not a popularity contest, and you can't be expected to hit it off with everyone—it may only take one deep connection to make all the difference to you and your career. So stay positive, review the steps outlined in this guide, move on to your next contact, and make sure you're on your best networking behavior.

Receptiveness to the possibilities. You never know whether you'll make a powerful connection at a conference, a friend's wedding, or a karate class. Stop relying on stock questions like "What do you do?" and "How do you know the bride?"; instead probe to find out what it is that inspires the people you meet most in their work and life. When you do, you might be surprised how much you share with and can learn from those around you. Don't limit your conversations to people whom you think might be immediately useful to you, either—that's downright distasteful, and not terribly forward-looking besides. Your fellow business school alum may not be willing or able to introduce you to the chief technical officer at his consulting firm, whereas your dry-cleaner might be on excellent terms with the CTO, as a longtime client, and offer to introduce you.

Generosity. Share your ideas and insights, and let your contacts know when you hear of job opportunities or fun events that might interest them. If you enjoy someone's company, let them know and do your best to make time for them even if your schedule is full. Take time out to introduce people who you think might share something in common, inviting them to events or dinner parties and putting them in touch via e-mail. Being generous makes you feel good, and it's a source of strength and comfort to know that there are people out there who think kindly of you and would probably be pleased to do you a good turn. Those you have helped are much more likely to think of you when they hear of a relevant work opportunity or meet someone in your desired field.

Success Signposts

How will you know whether you're on the right track? If you're on your best networking behavior and take the specific steps described in the chapters that follow, you should begin to see some subtle success indicators within a relatively short time. If you're able to meet with five to ten new people every month, you may begin to notice some subtle success indicators in a matter of months; if you're a less active networker, it will take longer to see evidence that you're networking effectively.

So, what are such signs?

- You should find that it's easier to connect not only with strangers, but also with people you thought you already knew intimately—friends, loved ones, even family.

- Positive contacts should become gradually more pronounced, and the less than positive ones should become easier to brush off.

- Listening should become second nature to you, and you may find people listen more closely when you are doing the talking.

Some longer-term indicators of successful networking:

- Your reputation as someone who is "good to know" will begin to get around, and you may find that you are more warmly received in professional and social circles.

- People whom you have never met personally know you by name or reputation.

To say that networking can increase your reach exponentially is an understatement—see "The X Factor: Becoming One in a Million through Networking" for an example of how successful networking can become the X factor in building a name for yourself.

The X Factor: Becoming One in a Million through Networking

1 ———▶ 1

Mingle: At a party, you hit it off with a friend of your sister's who is a real estate agent and seems to share your interest in art.

Make a date: You suggest meeting for lunch, and she enthusiastically agrees.

Explore common interests: Over lunch you learn that she's a freelance art critic on the side, so naturally you mention that you are an artist on the side—and that you may have a piece in an upcoming show at a local gallery.

Follow up: She asks you to keep her posted, and you send her an e-mail when the show is confirmed.

1 ———▶ 1 ———▶ 250,000

She comes to the show and reviews it in a major metropolitan paper with a readership of some 250,000 people, singling out your piece for praise. The review increases foot traffic to the gallery significantly, too.

1 ———▶ 1 ———▶ 250,000 ———▶ 1 million

A freelance curator who came by to check out the show after seeing the review calls and asks to visit your studio. When he does, he selects a piece for a show that travels to Los Angeles and Minneapolis. The show gets coverage in both cities, in newspapers with circulations of 650,000 and 350,000, respectively.

Working a Room, and Other Misconceptions

A timid young woman named Jane
Found parties a terrible strain;
With movements uncertain
She'd hide in a curtain
And make sounds like a rabbit in pain.

—*Edward Gorey*

If Edward Gorey's limerick strikes us as painfully funny, it's because there's a little bit of Jane in many of us. A lot of people avoid networking because they think of it as distasteful, difficult, or even a little sleazy. These objections may seem fair enough, but they're based on four pernicious misconceptions about networking.

1. "I'm too busy to network."

Many people don't like to admit that they're good at networking, because they're afraid that other people might think of them as slackers who spend their time chatting or plotting career moves instead of working. Networking is not a substitute for hard work, but it does make your hard work more visible and thus garners wider recognition for the work you do. If the idea of laboring in obscurity at the same job for years and years appeals to you, you can put this guide away now. But if you want your efforts to be acknowledged and rewarded in proportion to their merit, you need to ensure that others notice your performance and spread the good word.

As for the time-management aspect of this complaint, bear in mind that networking is also an invaluable time-saver. For example, if you're new at your job and are losing sleep over your first presentation to top executives, stop agonizing and start collecting pointers and constructive feedback from your network. If you're swamped with more work than one person can handle because of the company's hiring freeze, you can tap your network to find a capable intern to help—or help you make a case for a serious raise. And don't overlook the personal time and cost savings networking offers. A few questions may be all it takes to find competent child care, the correct part to resurrect your defunct printer, a reliable moving company, or someone to buy your old car, and perhaps most important for an overworked person such as yourself, a bargain plane fare for your long-overdue dream vacation to Bora Bora.

2. "I'm too shy to network."

You don't need to be all smiles and clever anecdotes to make a positive impression. On the contrary, some of the most effective networkers are those who listen thoughtfully and take genuine interest in others. This is a talent that shy people tend to cultivate better than gregarious types, who may have to rein in their instinct to pour on the charm and dominate conversations. So if you can get over that initial fear, shyness can actually be an advantage when it comes to networking.

3. "I hate crowds."

You don't need to work a room to be good at networking. Just get to know one person on his or her own merits, and try to find subjects that seem to bring out the best in that person. Seeing people light up is its own reward, but it also makes for a memorable interaction and might leave you with some valuable career and life lessons. If crowds make you downright claustrophobic, don't overlook the

multitude of online networking opportunities through professional forums or mail groups (see "Internet-Working" later in this chapter for more). But given that communication research shows that face-to-face interaction still cements a relationship like nothing else, you will eventually need to conquer any deep fears you may have that are not really about crowds *per se*, but actually about interpersonal social contact with others.[1] Career counselors, therapists, and public speaking coaches can be valuable allies in this process (see "The Fear Factor," following).

4. "I don't like being so fake."

If the term networking brings to mind forced laughter at the annual company picnic or secret alliances worthy of a reality TV show, think again. That isn't networking; that's phoniness, and it's no way to build a career or go through life, for that matter. (Sooner or later, that act is bound to wear thin for you and everyone around you.) Networking requires honesty, openness, and vulnerability. After all, you need to be willing to discuss your deepest hopes and interests, and you have to be open to input from others who may be able to help you reach your dreams. If you don't tell people what you really want, how can you possibly expect them to help you?

> I'd have this rule that nobody could do anything phony when they visited me.
> If anybody tried to do anything phony, they couldn't stay.
> —*J. D. Salinger* (from *The Catcher in the Rye*)

[1]Qingwen Dong. *Effective Employee/Supervisor Communication*. IABC Research Foundation, 2001.

The Fear Factor

Studies show that most Americans recognize that we have far less to fear from an awkward lunch than, say, illness, crime, accidents, fire, or attacks.[1] Yet even though we know that stilted conversation is easily reversible and leaves no visible scars, the fear of it can loom large in our imaginations. But not to worry: There are ways to shrink that fear to its appropriate size.

First, you must identify the source of your fear. Then, take concrete steps to address it.

Shyness

If you're shy, do whatever you have to do to get over your fear of that first meeting with a contact. This could be a simple matter of role-playing an informational interview with a friend or supportive colleague for that extra boost of confidence, inviting a friend you haven't seen in awhile to lunch to brush up on your small talk skills, hosting a mock-networking party with friends, or having a few people over for dinner to get more comfortable carrying a conversation. If a lingering fear of getting completely tongue-tied prevents you from taking any of these steps, you may feel more comfortable addressing the issue with a career counselor or therapist or enrolling in a public speaking class.

Fear of Rejection

If your fear of rejection is holding you back, have a list of desired initial contacts ready before you make the first phone call (or send the e-mail, etc.), so that if

[1] Peter D. Hart. Research Associates and Speakout.com press release, October 2001.

the first person you contact is not receptive to your invitation, you can just move on to the next person on your list.

If you get no response at first, you should ask again once or twice—voice mails, e-mails, and letters can always fall between the cracks—but after that, shift your time and energy to other contacts. When someone actually declines your invitation, accept the answer graciously. Don't ask why—just thank them politely for their time and move on.

Everyone gets ignored or turned down, so don't take it personally. In all likelihood, it has nothing to do with you. There are a multitude of reasons someone may have for declining that have nothing to do with you: deadlines, family commitments, health trouble, their own career crises, and so on.

Embarrassment

If you're so embarrassed by your current employment status—whether you're unemployed altogether (and perhaps have been for some time) or have a job that's not right for you (for whatever reason)—that you feel too demoralized to network, you're not alone. Many people have lost their jobs in the post-boom era, so the fear of unemployment is very present and real—which can make discussing career aims and prospects a potentially stressful conversation that many choose to avoid. But if you let your discomfort prevent you from pursuing your career aims, your fear could well become a self-fulfilling prophecy.

Although it might not be easy the first time you have to explain to a contact that you were laid off or are looking to make a significant career transition, your contact probably has friends, family, or colleagues who have been in a similar position, and he or she will likely understand where you're coming from and will admire your initiative. So, the next time you explain your aims you should find it less difficult, and by the tenth time it will be a piece of cake.

For support and encouragement, it often helps to talk to others who are in a similar position. Look for a local job search group or online mail list for job seekers. If you already know someone who shares your insecurities (e.g., a co-worker who was laid off at the same time), think about setting up a buddy system. Make a pact with your friend that you will each squeeze in just one extra meeting over lunch or coffee with a work or industry contact every week, and check up with one another on Fridays to see how it went that week. Stepping up your networking efforts together can strengthen the ties that bind you to your work, position you among the ranks of above-average job candidates in your field, provide the encouragement and sympathy you need to persevere, and be a bonding experience to boot.

Unsure of Your Goals

If you've been avoiding the subject of your career altogether, you'll first need to get comfortable talking about your career path and future direction. You can easily do so by first talking to friends and family about your work experience and your hopes and goals. In the process of talking with those who know you well, you will inevitably learn more about yourself and fine-tune your career goals. Be sure to do some research to learn more about your career options; you'll be much more comfortable discussing your professional goals when you are knowledgeable about the industry or field that you want to work in. Also consider talking to a licensed career counselor who can help you overcome your fears and find your focus.

Once you have identified your desired direction, try role-playing a networking meeting with a friend over coffee before you meet with a contact. Never underestimate the value of practice.

Your Network
(It's Bigger than You Think)

> No soul is desolate as long as there is a human being for
> whom it can feel trust and reverence.
> —*attributed to George Eliot*

You don't need to make nice with Donald Trump to have the proverbial golden Rolodex. Fact is, in your line of work there are probably far fewer than six degrees of separation. Through a single friend or colleague in the business, you may already be connected to a broad spectrum of professional peers and powers that be. So stop worrying about who you don't know, and concentrate on who you do know. Your existing and potential contacts fall into three broad categories, which we have described below just to get you thinking. In the next chapter, you'll work your way through each of these in detail.

Your Inner Circle

Your inner circle includes people who know you quite well:

- **Family, immediate and extended:** blood relatives, stepparents and step-siblings, adoptive and foster family members, and anyone else you've ever spent the holidays with.

- **Friends:** that is, anyone who would be happy to hear from you.

- **Colleagues, current and former:** anyone who knows you well in a professional capacity, including current and former co-workers, bosses, and consultants.

- **Classmates and professors:** especially those in your field.

- **Activity partners:** anyone you've bonded with over daily routines, common interests, or shared personal beliefs (e.g., religious or political convictions).

If you're not sure whether someone belongs in your inner circle, ask yourself this question: If I ran into this person on the street, would I stop to talk? If your feelings about a person aren't strong enough to merit a "Hi, what's new?" or you're not sure the person would welcome the overture, that person is probably not part of your inner circle and will probably not be your strongest contact.

Your Extended Network

Your extended network consists of all the people with whom you've had contact or met (but who aren't a part of your inner circle):

- **Acquaintances:** anyone who'd recognize you in the street. This includes people you were introduced to in social settings and people you may have had brief contact with professionally. This might include people you seriously considered hiring as employees or consultants or who interviewed you at one point and were favorably impressed, even though the position turned out not to be an exact match for your talents or interests, for example.

- **Fellow association members:** this includes professional, community, or alumni associations (see "Networking Around the World").

- **Regular e-mail correspondents and fellow online community members:** including fellow participants in an e-mail group or community forum.

- **People you know by reputation:** people your friends, family, or colleagues have brought up in the course of conversation.

In other words, your extended network includes anyone who would say "Ah, yes!" when you mention the connection between you. Generally speaking, anyone in this group should be receptive to your invitation to lunch or coffee.

Networking Around the World

One of the most effective networks in the world is the one organized by returned Peace Corps volunteers. "RPCVs" say they consider strength of character and resourcefulness to be the hallmarks of any RPCV, and they consider it their duty to assist any other RPCV to the best of their ability. (One RPCV claims she's landed every job she's ever had through her RPCV connections.) They've even founded their own nonprofit organization (www.rpcv.org), which members can use to:

- Find some 300 people in the Hospitality Network who are willing to put them up while traveling
- Participate in one of the 140 affiliate groups nationwide
- Connect to thousands of RPCVs through reunions, conferences, and events
- Qualify for grants to fund community-based development projects
- Find a ready-made network of other RPCVs eager to help them find meaningful work overseas and Stateside

The Network You Never Knew You Had

Strange but true: You may not yet have had personal contact with all of your contacts. These heretofore unknown and potential contacts may include:

- **Friends, relatives, and colleagues of friends, relatives, and colleagues:** Boggles the mind, doesn't it? There's a whole host of people out there who may be willing to meet with you based on your mutual connection. So even if you don't have any friends, relatives, or colleagues in your chosen field, you can always cast a wider net by asking these people if they have any personal or professional connections to people in your field and would be willing to refer you. In the next chapter (see "Where to Cast Your Net"), we'll show you which friends, relatives, and colleagues are most likely to yield the most useful contacts.

- **Fans of your work:** If you've ever given lectures or led a workshop, published an article or book, or created your own website or e-mail newsletter, odds are you have contacts you've overlooked or forgotten about. You can count as contacts registered users on your personal website, co-workers in distant divisions of your company, people who have signed up for your mailing list, anyone who has sent you fan mail or a thank-you note for your work, and anyone else who has expressed familiarity (positively, of course) with your work.

- **Public figures in your chosen field:** People who have received a certain level of prominence in any field know that they may be contacted by people who read articles and books by or about them or have heard them at lectures, on the radio, or on TV. If you ask specific questions nicely enough, they may be inclined to respond.

With people who are one step removed from you, there's always a chance they might draw a blank and say "I'm sorry?" after you explain your connection. Don't let this stop you—just press on, and introduce yourself on your own merits. Nothing makes a bad situation worse (and more embarrassing for everyone involved) than a comeback like, "You don't know who I am?" or "Haven't you heard about me?" So come prepared to introduce yourself with the elevator pitch you'll work out in the next chapter.

Internet-Working

If you're not already active on the Internet, now is the time to start. You can find all manner of career advice and points of connection online and seek out still more through select blogs, postings, and e-mail. But don't just wallpaper the Web with your words—think carefully about every post and e-mail before you press send, since these will be your online calling cards. When contacts who don't know you personally Google your name to find out more about you before they commit to lunch, you want to be sure that they don't find anything that might reflect poorly on you.

Using the Web to Find Career Opportunities

The Web can be useful in determining where to focus your career development efforts. If you're not sure where the opportunities in your field lay, you can pore over the labor market projections and statistics on the U.S. Bureau of Labor Statistics' site (www.bls.gov), WetFeet's site (www.wetfeet.com), and NaceWeb (www.naceweb.org). But you might be better off doing a search on Google to track down the professional association websites and online trade publications for your field to find out what insights they have to offer. Many trade publications and association newsletters run a special issue every year on the state of the industry, complete with salary surveys, sample job descriptions, and opportunity analyses—you're not the only one who's interested in this information!

But even the best statistical estimates are no substitute for personal insight, so you'll want to find contacts in your field who may be able to shed some light on

the subject. Try asking these questions in e-mail discussion groups and community forums:

- I recently read that [industry name] is one of the fastest-growing fields. Judging from your experience, is there an area where you expect particularly strong growth in the next few years?

- I've heard that the demand for experienced [position title] is on the rise. Do you think this holds true in your workplace? Do you expect that to last?

- I know that [industry] was pretty hard hit this year. How long do you think it will take the industry to recover? Are there any industry niches you think are likely to rebound first?

- I notice that the turnover rates are pretty high for [position]. That position looks pretty attractive to me—is there something I don't know about?

But, Don't Get Caught in the Web

Many people make the mistake of not paying attention to their presence online, so this could be a competitive advantage for you. To make a positive impression online, you'll want to avoid these common errors.

Sending flames and rants. Think twice before you call anyone a pea-brain, incompetent, or worse in an online forum, or go on a tirade about men, women, kids these days, Baby Boomers, Luddites, or any of the other usual suspects people tend to rant about. Do you really want to be known as someone who's a hothead, impatient, intolerant, or a bigot? If you do choose to share an opinion about a political, social, or religious issue, be sure you state your opinion logically and succinctly and explain the reasoning behind your opinion. Same goes for criticism of a particular film, book, albums, show, or artist. People feel passionately about their favorite artists, and some people who will tolerate measured challenges to their political and religious beliefs will never forgive you for making a flippant comment about Elvis.

Forgetting where you are. Give some thought to where you post and blog—if you're going to share your, er, thoughts on a sex site, the bulletin board for some cheesy TV show, or the notorious F*cked Company website, you might want to use a pseudonym. The Web is a public forum, and things you say among friends in the privacy of your living room are not always appropriate there.

Using your main e-mail address for all posts. You think you get spam now? Just wait until you start using your business or primary personal e-mail address to post in online forums and mail groups. And all you need is one hacker or wacko to get hold of your e-mail address to make life difficult. Check the spam policies for the online forums and mail groups you participate in before you post, and set up a separate e-mail account with spam-blocking capabilities as a repository for responses to your posts.

Being a joker. If you like to share jokes online, post outrageous comments just to see the reaction, or fill your posts with smiley-face emoticons, you may want to use a handle—and even then, watch yourself. You may love to make people laugh, but you also want prospective employers and professional contacts to take you seriously. Some people might not find your comments all that funny, and without the nonverbal cues of a wink and a nudge, some may misconstrue your meaning. A crack you make in an online forum about liking your men barefoot and pregnant might linger there in the archives for years to come and may come back to haunt you.

Avoid these errors and build your online presence through the outlets described below, and your name will soon be associated with Google search results that'll do you proud.

Mail Groups

Mail groups are like online coffee klatches, usually started by groups of people with a common interest who want to share questions, ideas, and information on that subject. There's a mail group for every conceivable professional and personal interest, from nanotechnology to impersonating Peter Pan. You may have to be invited to join the group by an existing member or you may have to be approved by a moderator before you can join, which makes these groups somewhat more exclusive than online forums. Your listserv may thus provide an entrée to professionals who are advanced and well regarded in your field, who you might not otherwise have a chance to meet in a peer-to-peer setting.

Well-selected mail groups can be instrumental in your career in a number of ways. First of all, many employers prefer to post jobs on professionally vetted discussion groups rather than on general-interest sites or newspapers, which tend to elicit a high volume of responses from unqualified candidates. So, you may very well hear of opportunities through your mail group that aren't posted elsewhere. You can also post messages to solicit expert advice on specific questions related to your job and career, such as how to handle a new responsibility you've taken on, pointers for tackling a tricky problem, or background on a particular company where you think you'd like to work. Your questions and responses to others' questions may impress your fellow group members and contribute to your professional reputation. These responses may be archived, so that when prospective employers Google your name they can see your responses—all the more reason to make sure you look good online.

Many people are very loyal to their mail groups and are receptive to fellow members who approach them about a specific work-related issue "off-list," in a personal e-mail. That said, don't assume it's OK to push just any personal agenda through your mail group. Most groups expressly forbid using the group for e-mail

harvesting, which is the practice of collecting e-mail addresses in order to send out mass mailings or solicitations for your business services. You could get banned from the group for this, and blacklisted as a spammer besides. Once you're blacklisted, your e-mails may be blocked from getting through by many Internet providers, and it can be very difficult to get yourself unlisted so that your e-mails will reach their intended recipients.

Ask people in your field or areas of interest to suggest mail groups that they've found active, on-topic, and helpful, or ask on community sites if anyone can recommend an appropriate site given your needs and interests. But don't expect everyone to be forthcoming with invitations to join their discussion group. Just as people can be reluctant to share contacts they value highly, some people value "their" list for the exclusive access it may provide to influential people in their field, as well as the advanced nature of the discussions—too many newbies, they might claim, and the list becomes less useful to advanced practitioners. As a last resort, run a Web search with the search parameter "listserv+[name of your field]", and if you come up with thousands of possibilities add your geographic region or area of specialization.

Community Forums

Online community forums are similar to neighborhood rec centers and other community organizations. Some are professionally oriented, while others are primarily social—but all are helpful in expanding your networking efforts. Community forums give you a chance to meet people from all over the world who share your professional and/or personal interests, and they provide a "place" where you can chat, schmooze, learn more about fields you'd like to enter, and sometimes peruse subject-specific job postings that you're not likely to see on general-interest job sites or in newspapers.

Follow the advice above for mail groups to find community forums in your areas of interest, but also poke around to find the best community forums in your region. Some community forums provide listings of mixers, professional gatherings, citywide treasure hunts, and other events where you can get to know people in a relaxed environment. Craigslist (www.craigslist.com), Citysearch (www.citysearch.com), and Digital City (www.digitalcity.com) are three popular community sites with several locations around the United States. In addition to helping you find dates and garage sales, these sites can hook you up with everything from CPA positions to cartooning gigs—one freelance graphic designer claims he's landed every gig he's gotten in the past five years through Craigslist.

The more specific you can be about your interests, the better—odds are, you'll find like-minded people out there with whom you can network. Check out Meetup (www.meetup.com), the 2003 Webby "Best Community Site" winner that organizes local interest groups ranging from Elvis Presley fans in Brisbane, Australia, to stay-at-home moms in Raleigh, North Carolina. World travelers flock to Thorn Tree (http://thorntree.lonelyplanet.com), where they can seek advice or find traveling partners for especially arduous journeys (misery loves company).

There are many community forums that give people a chance to express themselves creatively and connect at the same time. Blog sites (short for "Web log") give you the chance to put your thoughts on the Web map and invite responses via return e-mail. Two popular blog sites are LiveJournal (www.livejournal.com) and Blog-Spot (www.blogspot.com). Most blog sites don't archive entries older than a month, though, so don't expect to impress people with dazzling prose you blogged six months ago. Memories are short in the world of blogging, so people tend to remember you by current blog. Those with creative mojo to spare may enjoy Nervousness.org (http://nervousness.org/index.php), where you can start or add to an art project that gets mailed around the world.

Of course, in any community forum you're likely to meet a few people who claim to be there to pursue a specific interest, but whose ulterior motive is to meet people to date. If there are more than a few people who are flirting online, this may not be the best place to pursue your career interests. If discussions on an ostensibly engineering-focused site seem to be persistently rife with innuendo about hard drives, for example, you might take it as a hint that you'd be better off directing your questions about the future in nanotechnology elsewhere. Always check out any site carefully before you jump into the fray, and think before you send—people may well judge you by the company you keep online.

Personal Website

You also might want to create your own website that reflects your interests, creativity, and personality to set yourself apart from countless others out there and attract new contacts. To get a sense of what sets a personal website apart from the crowd, take a look at the Webby nominees for best personal site at www.webbyawards.com. True story: One amateur robot-builder's site had such creative, helpful tips for other robotics enthusiasts that it eventually attracted the attention of Disney, who hired him as one of their elite Imagineers. His site had all the key personal site elements needed to establish him as an expert in his subject and as a creative, likable guy:

- An original, attractive design
- Useful, engaging content describing key aspects and exciting developments in his field, written in a way that even nonexperts could understand
- A great bio page that briefly told the story of his interest in his field, outlined his most exciting current projects, and described aspects of the field that seemed most promising to him and that he'd like to pursue in the future
- Plenty of places where he solicited feedback, ideas, and questions from visitors— all of which were sent to a single blind e-mail address to minimize spam.

But before you rush right out and invest considerable time and/or cash in Web design, content, engineering, and hosting, consider the possible return. Yes, Disney is trolling the Web for prospective Imagineers, but not every industry is so Web-focused. How likely are people in, say, the insurance industry to even glance at your personal site? And keep in mind that you may actually limit your options if your job search is fairly broad and your website is not. If you're applying for jobs as a real estate agent and your personal website is all about your passion for acting, you might confuse your prospective employers from real estate agencies who visit the site. If your career track is not so narrowly defined and (like most Americans) you've had a career change or two, it's probably wise to omit your resume on the site so that you can tailor it to the job at hand, and instead write a bio for the site that is more reflective of all your career interests and pursuits. That way, prospective employers are more likely to think of you as well rounded than as potentially schizophrenic.

Networking Sites

In the last few years, social-networking sites have become much more common—and popular. The jury is still out regarding the effectiveness of these sites, however, and it's worth taking the time to find out which sites are right (or wrong) for you and your goals. Although many of these networking sites are aimed at nonprofessional networking, that doesn't mean that they can't play a role in your career development. After all, your friends make up an enormous part of your network.

Through a single connection on a social-networking site like Friendster (www.friendster.com) or Tribe.net (www.tribe.net), which are not limited to professional networking, you may be automatically linked to thousands of people. Most networking sites make your intentions and interests known, so that you can search for people (and people can search for you) according to

occupation, favorite book, and so on. One woman in California located a long-lost friend in Ethiopia on Friendster.com and found out that through him she was one step removed from a member of the Grateful Dead—so she now has standing invites to Addis Ababa and reunion tours.

For those who are strictly business, there's Ryze (http://new.ryze.com/index.php), a 2003 Forbes Favorite Award winning networking site for business professionals, and LinkedIn (www.linkedin.com). But don't limit yourself to staid business sites for networking—some people have had impressive professional results from other "purely social" sites, too (see "It Could Happen to You: Going Global").

Networking sites give you an opportunity to mingle with geographically dispersed contacts who you might never have had a chance to meet face to face—and this has its pluses and minuses. If you're thinking about relocating to a new place, or traveling for work or pleasure to a distant locale, you might already have contacts there through your virtual connections. On the other hand, most virtual interactions are free of interpersonal cues, and it can be hard to gauge someone's truthfulness, motives, sense of humor, ethics, and mental stability without even being able to look into that person's eyes. So if you do have an opportunity to meet someone you hit it off with online, plan to meet in a public space where you feel safe and can excuse yourself and disappear into a crowd quickly if you are made to feel uncomfortable or threatened in any way. Some networking sites have prearranged rendezvouses, where you can meet and mingle in a larger group; this is probably your safest bet for a first meeting with online contacts.

It Could Happen to You: Going Global

Lest you ever be tempted to forget about distant connections and stick close to home and within your industry for contacts, consider this true story of networking with global reach.

When a cellular technology engineer (and particularly adept networker) from Bangalore had a business trip planned to San Francisco, he tracked down his professor cousin in North Carolina and got the number of a nonprofit manager friend of hers in San Francisco. Then the programmer invited the cousin's friend and her artist husband for coffee. They all hit it off, so the couple showed him the local sights, including a show of the husband's artwork, and remained friends after he returned to India. As a founding member of a social-networking site, the programmer recommended to his online circle that they keep an eye out for art shows by this promising artist he'd just met. An agent in Boston took note and now represents the artist.

Mapped geographically, here's how that connection would look:

Bangalore ——→ San Francisco ——→ Networking Site ——→ Boston

Mapped in terms of industries covered, here's how that would look:

Cellular technology ——→ Academia ——→ Nonprofit ——→ Arts ——→ Agent

What's the moral of this story? Never assume that contacts within your industry or city are inherently more valuable than those in other fields or countries. Reach out to others with the help of the Internet, and you might find good friends and esteemed colleagues all over the world.

Gain Advantage without Taking Advantage

> "Before I can live with other folks I've got to live with myself. The one thing
> that doesn't abide by majority rule is a person's conscience."
>
> —*Harper Lee* (from *To Kill a Mockingbird*)

Many people would sooner admit to stealing kids' candy at Halloween than networking because there are people out there giving networking a bad name. There are pyramid schemers, Hollywood B-movie producers, ersatz Enron-style executives, and other con artists who talk a mile a minute, pushing their marks into doing something ill-advised or illegal. These flimflammers may consider themselves experts in working a connection, but don't be fooled, and certainly don't follow their lead.

First of all, misrepresenting yourself or the facts to establish a contact or extract what you want from a contact is unethical, and possibly fraudulent. Second, tricking or badgering people into helping you tends to backfire. You might be able to trick or badger someone into helping you one time, but the odds are that no one involved is going to feel particularly good about it afterward—not your contact, not the friends and family who vouch for your integrity, and certainly not you. Sooner or later someone will see through your act and discover hidden motives. Networking works best when you take genuine personal interest in your contact— not just what that contact can do for you.

With networking your goal is to build bridges, not burn them. One of the best ways you can do this is to help others out—it boosts your reputation as someone who is useful to know, and it's always good to have a few favors you can call in when the going gets tough. But most important, it feels good! Do what is right by law and your conscience, and you'll earn yourself a name to be proud of— not one that consists of four letters.

First Steps

- Define Your Direction

- Get Equipped

- Where to Cast Your Net

- Prepare Your Approach

- Make the Approach

- How to Handle Referrals

Define Your Direction

Before you start pursuing contacts in earnest, you need to be prepared to sum up your career direction in one sentence. Yes, that's *one sentence*—the perfect length for your initial introduction to a new contact, whether it's in an e-mail, on a phone call, or in person. You'll want to memorize this sentence so that you're always prepared to succinctly and convincingly answer the question, "What kind of work are you looking for?" If you have to remember more than one sentence, you'll start forgetting and stumble over your words. If the listener is interested in knowing more about you, he or she will ask. In that case, you are free to engage in a discussion that reflects the listener's level of interest. But remember, you're here to learn everything you can from your contacts, not to take center stage.

Defining your direction in a single sentence may require some soul-searching, but that doesn't mean you sit on a mountaintop and wait for a revelation. Just find the description that best characterizes your situation in the sections that follow and, using the tips provided, spend some time reflecting on your past as well as on your future.

When you're ready, use the Define Your Direction workbook to draft your own one-sentence explanation of your career aspirations.

Just Starting Out

If you're a recent grad or otherwise relatively new to the job market, you might not think you have much to say about your career direction yet. Fiddlesticks! Isn't there a specific subject that excited you in school? Have you ever taken an

internship, volunteer position, or summer job because you thought the work sounded worthwhile? Think about how you might combine the best of each of those experiences in a job, because this combination of interests and skills will help set you apart. And, don't be afraid to talk to friends and family to help you consider your direction.

Then, think about how you might fill in the blanks in this sentence:

"I studied/worked in _____, which was great because it allowed me to hone my skills in _____—but I also particularly enjoyed _____, so I'm excited to learn more about how I might make use of my abilities in _____ while pursuing my interests in _____ as a _____."

For example: "I studied child psychology and education in college, which was great because it allowed me to hone my skills in age-appropriate lesson planning—but I also particularly enjoyed model U.N. in high school, so I'm excited to learn more about how I might make use of my abilities in curriculum development while pursuing my interests in public policy as an educational policy lobbyist."

After you've thought about how your interests, experience, and education have influenced your career aspirations and you've talked to friends and family to solidify those thoughts, it's time to craft your one-sentence explanation, in the Define Your Direction workbook. You may want to use the sample sentence format shown above, or you may want to rewrite the sentence to better reflect your particular situation.

But, before you start, here's a tip especially for those of you just starting out. You can get the edge on a lot of networking newbies out there by avoiding these three phrases in describing your career direction:

"I've always dreamed of being a _____." Don't utter this phrase unless you really mean it. Americans switch careers several times, so it's perfectly fine to say you always thought you were going to be a farmer like your dad until you saw *Citizen Kane* a couple years ago and decided you wanted to make films. And don't pretend to yourself—or anyone else—that you've always dreamed of being a dental hygienist, if what you're really after is a job you know you're good at with decent pay, nice people, and a flexible schedule so you can shoot your first movie in your downtime. If your prospective employer is gullible enough to be duped into hiring you, then you'll have to spend 40 hours a week faking it and secretly dreaming of the silver screen. Being honest allows you to sleep at night, and it can also set you apart from the other candidates. One aspiring artist who is honest about his artistic pursuits has attained the Holy Grail of sought-after, well-paid, flexible part-time positions, with employers in other fields who also happen to be art lovers eager to have a kindred spirit and creative energy in the workplace.

"I don't really have any experience." Experience doesn't have to be paid. It may include your studies, volunteer work, nonacademic activities, or internships. If you've already spent two years studying dental hygiene and interning at a dentist's office, you definitely have experience. If you shot a short film for a class project about volunteer work dentists have done for uninsured patients in need of major reconstructive surgery, you have a jumpstart in a career in film, too. You don't need to overstate your experience, but there's no sense in negating it entirely.

"I haven't figured out what I want to do yet." Then why are you taking up your contact's valuable time?! Before you talk to your contact, make a list of things you most enjoy doing and think of careers that might allow you to pursue those interests. If you're still stuck, talk to a career counselor—many offer diagnostic career tests—to come up with a list of jobs you're likely to find satisfying. Talk

to your friends, family, and peers about your dilemma, too. Your nearest and dearest may be best able to identify your strengths; they may also be able to recall times when you excelled at or particularly enjoyed something new and thus steer you toward fields where you are sure to shine.

Define Your Direction: In One Sentence

Once you've found the section that describes your situation ("Just Starting Out," "Changing Careers," or "Getting Ahead") and followed the tips provided there, thought about how your interests, education, and experience have influenced your career aspirations, and talked to friends, family, or anyone else who might have insight, it's time to craft your one-sentence explanation.

Note: You may choose to use the sample sentence format provided in the text, or you may choose to rewrite the sentence to better reflect your particular situation.

_____

_____

_____

_____

_____

_____

In the course of networking, as you learn more about the field or position that you're interested in, you'll likely want to make changes (or rewrite altogether) the sentence above from time to time. That's good—that means you're getting closer to finding the right path!

Changing Careers

If you want to switch from one industry or career to another, think about what has inspired your thoughts of a career change. Was it a satisfying volunteer gig? Having your first child? Discovering through experience that although insurance billing pays better, you still really miss teaching? What specific area excites you most in the field you're eager to move into?

Think about how you might fill in the blanks in this sentence:

"So far I've been a _____, which has been good because it allowed me to _____—but after _____, I realize that _____, and I'm excited to learn more about _____ in particular."

For example: "So far I've been a graphic designer, which has been good because it has definitely sharpened my ability to convey messages through visual imagery—but after seeing the amazing set for Cirque du Soleil's O, I realize that set design is the ultimate visual problem-solving challenge, and I'm excited to learn more about lighting design in particular."

Once you've thought about how your interests and experience have influenced your decision to pursue a new career direction, it's time to craft your one-sentence explanation, in the Define Your Direction workbook.

Getting Ahead

If you already have a sense of what you want to accomplish in your career, your peers and mentors can help you shape those lifelong ambitions into achievable goals. You'll need to be able to talk about what you like about your current or last position, especially as it relates to your desired position, as well as about why you want to move in the direction you do.

Think about how you might fill in the blanks in this sentence:

"_____ has been good to me so far, and I really enjoy _____—but I would like to become a _____ one day so that I can _____, and I'm not sure what steps I need to take to get there from here."

For example: "Accounting has been good to me so far, and I really enjoy the satisfaction of knowing I've solved concrete problems at the end of the day—but I would like to become a CFO one day so that I can actually prevent financial problems instead of fixing them on the back end, and I'm not sure what steps I need to take to get there from here."

Once you've identified why you want to make the change you do and you understand how that goal is informed by your experience, it's time to craft your one-sentence explanation, in the Define Your Direction workbook.

Get Equipped

As with all major projects, using the right tools can make all the difference. The right networking tools will yield the best results and help you make the most of your time. And nothing projects professionalism and competence better than being organized and prepared. There are a few tools you can use to help you make the most of your networking efforts. Just as you wouldn't set out to build a house with just a hammer, you'll need much more than a pad of scratch paper to build your network.

Business Cards

Business cards are networking essentials—no matter where you go, don't leave home without them. Whether you already have a job or are in between jobs, business cards remind people who you are, what business you're in, and convey your professionalism. If a contact of yours meets someone in your line of work who is in need of your services, your contact can pass your business card along immediately—instant gratification! And, you know that the correct information is provided—your name is spelled correctly, your phone number and e-mail address are current and typo-free, and your line of work is identified just as you intend (as opposed, for example, to "my friend, the web designer" when you're really a web *developer*).

In particular, if you're going to a conference, traveling abroad, or attending any formal function, you risk appearing less than professional if you neglect to bring business cards. Just make a habit of toting a few cards with you everywhere, including cafés, parties, concerts, and gallery openings, because you never know

where you might meet someone who shares your interests, strikes you as an intriguing person, or is a potentially useful contact—or knows someone who is.

Business cards are the leave-behinds your contacts will have to remember you by, so you should make them distinctive and provide as much contact info as you can. You can get decent business cards designed and printed by a fancy letterpress printer, graphic design studio, or silk screener if you're really flush, an independent graphic designer or printer if you have a little less to spend, or your local Kinko's if you want to keep your costs as modest as possible.

Just don't wait around for the perfect business card forever. One nonprofit professional was caught between business cards when he left his position for grad school, not realizing that until he got set up he could have a business card from his school with his school e-mail address and cell phone number. As fate would have it, he met someone in his field at a party and ended up writing his number on a scrap of paper, which was promptly stuffed into the contact's jeans pocket and seemed fated to wind up in the wash. Don't let this happen to you!

Date Book

Since you'll soon be networking up a storm, you'll need a date book to make sure you don't make any double bookings. Keeping a date book around at all times is a wise networking idea—that way, when someone suggests lunch at the baseball game or PTO (parent-teacher organization) meeting, you can make a tentative plan right then and there. Having your schedule on hand also allows you to reschedule on the spot whenever necessary, without having to play phone tag. Don't feel like you need to have a big Filofax or slick Palm Pilot—the point is to have a schedule on hand that's portable and convenient enough that you can (and will) check every day. If you do go with a PDA, be sure you back up your data daily so you don't miss an appointment because your battery ran down and you lost data.

Wardrobe

Clean and simple business casual attire is the way to go when you're attending meetings. Unless you're coming directly from your workplace where you're expected to wear one, suits are to be avoided. Most networking meetings are over lunch or coffee and do not entail a formal interview. Besides, showing up in an Armani suit when you're meeting a homeless shelter administrator to talk about careers helping the needy could inspire some serious skepticism about your ability to comprehend poverty.

Adding a little of your own personality to your business-casual ensemble may not be a bad idea, though, especially if it gives you a boost of confidence. One woman swears by a lucky wrap she wears to meetings, saying it makes her feel more memorable and comfortable. But the point is that you want people to remember you, not your outrageous getup. One research firm executive recalls being completely distracted by the red rubber wading boots one librarian chose to wear to their lunch meeting on a clear day to discuss a career in research. Those boots sent a strong signal to the executive: This librarian is not really ready for the corporate world.

Even when attending social events, the networking-minded would do well to wear clothing that's relatively clean (unless you're playing soccer in the mud) and not too revealing (unless you're Britney Spears). You don't want people to be distracted from your friendly overtures and brilliant insights by your stench or appearance.

Work Samples

You probably won't want to whip these out should you meet a potential contact at a friend's dinner party, though some enterprising entrepreneurs have been known to carry work samples everywhere, ready to display them at the least

provocation. But, you should have work samples ready for a lunch meeting (but don't pull them out unless it's relevant to do so—there's no need to show someone examples of your design work if you're trying to move into human resources) or to send upon request. Recent is better, but you can dust off a few oldies but goldies if you must.

Your work samples should illustrate what an asset you can be, so don't just fire them off by e-mail without any explanation. Make sure you include a brief story (three sentences max) about the problem the project was intended to solve and how it met and exceeded expectations. Naturally, you should have this story prepared in advance, too. You knew we were going to say that, didn't you?

Resume

You don't need a perfectly polished resume in order to network—that's the oldest procrastination excuse in the book! You should be tailoring your resume to anticipate the demands of each job that comes your way, so there really is no such thing as the ideal one-size-fits-all resume. Besides, you run the risk of seeming a little forward by bringing your resume to a lunch meeting, unless you have asked your contact in advance if he or she would be willing to give you some tips for enhancing it.

If your contacts want your resume, they will ask for it—at which point you can offer to e-mail it to them. For this, you need to be sure to have a resume template ready that outlines your job experience, major accomplishments on each job, educational background, and language and technical skills. That way, you can quickly tailor it to anticipate your contact's needs and fire it off via e-mail.

Where to Cast Your Net

Now it's time to quickly draw up a list of contacts that will make up your network. Note the use of the qualifier *quickly*. Don't spend so much time coming up with thousands of contacts that you never get around to actually setting up a single meeting. Instead, try coming up with a list of possible contacts off the top of your head—no research allowed for this initial pass. From this list, you'll cull a short list of a few contacts to approach for lunch. Don't worry about coming up with a master list of 500 people; start with just five contacts in each category.

We walk you through this process step-by-step in the pages that follow. We've provided space for you to list contacts in the workbook immediately following this section, but you may also want to prepare an electronic text file or spreadsheet to record and organize this information. Note: We've included space for contact info, but that can be added later, if you don't have it handy.

You can return to this list later if need be, when you've exhausted your initial list or if you had trouble identifying people in one of the categories. Of course you'll add to this list as you expand your networking efforts and meet new people who introduce you to still more people.

Fishing in a Bathtub: Your Friends and Family

First things first: people you already know well, who may have some contact (however tangential) to fields that interest you.

Family. Obviously, you'll list your mother and father and any siblings, but you should extend this to include anyone you've ever spent a holiday with:

grandparents, aunts, uncles, cousins, in-laws, honorary uncles or aunts that are close friends of a parent—you get the idea.

Friends. List current friends, but also people you haven't been in touch with for awhile but who would probably be glad to hear from you: college buddies, former teammates, friends and neighbors you grew up with, people you pal around with at your favorite local haunts, anyone you've received a holiday card from in the last five years.

Professional and academic colleagues. This category runs the gamut from coworkers and vendors you see often to people you served with on a one-time task force, project, or presentation—basically, anyone who knows you in a professional capacity.

For current or recent students, you'll also want to include professors and fellow students who may have a connection to the field or industry you are targeting.

Activity partners. Think of every activity you do outside of work, and the odds are you can think of at least one person you've gotten to know there: people at your Italian class, your place of worship, the local café, the gym, the childcare center or playground where you take your kids, your favorite music venue, the organization where you volunteer delivering meals to the elderly, your favorite stores and restaurants, your local PTA, and so on.

When you're done, you should have a nice long list of personal contacts. These are the people who form the backbone of your network.

Your Inner Circle

List five contacts in each of the following categories, using the criteria provided in the text.

Family

Name	Contact info	Profession
_____	_____	_____
_____	_____	_____
_____	_____	_____
_____	_____	_____
_____	_____	_____

Friends

Name	Contact info	Profession
_____	_____	_____
_____	_____	_____
_____	_____	_____
_____	_____	_____
_____	_____	_____

Professional and Academic Colleagues

Name	Contact info	Profession
_____	_____	_____
_____	_____	_____
_____	_____	_____
_____	_____	_____
_____	_____	_____

Activity Partners

Name	Contact info	Profession
_____	_____	_____
_____	_____	_____
_____	_____	_____
_____	_____	_____
_____	_____	_____

First Steps

Fishing in a Pond: Your Extended Network

Next, rack your brains a little, and come up with a list of people in your chosen field who fall into one of the following subcategories.

Acquaintances. This is a catchall that includes anyone who might recognize you on the street—someone you've been introduced to at a social event, maybe, or know by name from your neighborhood. Friends of friends often fall into this category, as do people who work in other divisions of your company or organization with whom you occasionally have contact.

Fellow association members. If you don't belong to a professional, community, or alumni association already, now's the time to think about joining. A single association can offer multiple points of connection: professional mixers, conferences, online community forum discussions, affiliate interest group interactions, lectures, fundraisers, volunteer committee meetings, mentoring programs, and board of trustees retreats. Get more active in your alumni network or student group, and ask around or search online to find reputable professional organizations in your field as well as community organizations like the Rotary Club in your region or neighborhood.

E-mail correspondents and fellow online community members. If you're already e-mailing someone or participating in the same online mail group or community forum, you probably already have a foundation of shared interests to build from, and you may have a sense of that person's personality from their posts. True, not everyone is who they seem in writing—but it couldn't hurt to strike up a friendly conversation online or suggest meeting during the day in a busy, public place to discover what you might have in common. Be clear from the outset that you are looking for a purely platonic relationship.

People known to you by reputation. Does a friend of yours tell great anecdotes about a musician friend, or do you have a colleague who raves about the real estate agent who found a bargain? If you're looking to break into the music biz or find an affordable house, you should definitely ask to come along to the next show or ask for an introduction to the agent. The odds are your friend would be happy to bring a new fan into the fold, and send business in the direction of the effective agent.

Your Extended Network

List five contacts in each of the following categories, using the criteria provided in the text.

Acquaintances

Name	Contact info	Profession
_____	_____	_____
_____	_____	_____
_____	_____	_____
_____	_____	_____
_____	_____	_____

Your Extended Network (cont'd)

Fellow Association Members

Name	Contact info	Profession
_____	_____	_____
_____	_____	_____
_____	_____	_____
_____	_____	_____
_____	_____	_____

E-Mail Correspondents and Fellow Online Community Members

Name	Contact info	Profession
_____	_____	_____
_____	_____	_____
_____	_____	_____
_____	_____	_____
_____	_____	_____

Your Extended Network (cont'd)

People Known to You by Reputation

Name	Contact info	Profession
_____	_____	_____
_____	_____	_____
_____	_____	_____
_____	_____	_____
_____	_____	_____

Deep Sea Fishing: The Network You Never Knew You Had

By now you've probably amassed an impressive list of people. Your list might include a few contacts who are in your line of work or even some who could be in a position to help or hire you. That's great—but don't make a rookie's mistake and limit your networking to the obvious suspects! Even if you don't know many people in your line of work, you probably know people who do. Just do a little detective work, and you'll discover a network you never knew you had.

How can you track down these elusive contacts, you ask? Try consulting people from the following groups to help you in your quest. It's time to kick it into high gear and come up with at least a couple of contacts to approach from these sources. That gives you even more contacts to invite for lunch or coffee—go get 'em, tiger!

Friends who have professional dealings in your field. This refers to friends who are not actually in your chosen field but whose work may bring them into contact with other people in that field. For example, you may not know anyone who works in public relations, but you might have a friend whose job includes managing her company's relationship with its PR agency. It's worth asking whether she'd be willing to introduce you to her contact at the agency. But be sensitive to the fact that there may be extenuating circumstances that prevent even the most well-meaning friends from putting you in touch with people they know professionally.

Friends whose line of work requires them to have contact with a wide range of professions are an invaluable resource. Professionals that fall under this rubric include entrepreneurs, recruiters, journalists, salespeople, and PR pros.

Highly social friends. Anyone who has a wide social circle or who travels in many different social circles can probably think of at least one person in your line of work and will likely be willing to introduce you to each other. So just ask!

Resourceful friends. If you can't think of how to reach a particularly influential person in your field, remember that two heads are better than one, and ask a friend to help you come up with ideas. Since influential people tend to be well connected, there may be multiple points of contact through which you might reach them—so you and your friend should be able to come up with at least a couple of approaches.

Your fan base. You might not know them, but if you have published articles or books, circulated an e-mail newsletter, given lectures, or developed your own website, you may have fans out there who would be more than happy to talk to you. With every public appearance, include an e-mail address where people can send comments and feedback. And if you think of an issue you'd like input on or help in a specific area, include it in your next public address.

The Network You Never Knew You Had

List five contacts in each of the following categories, using the criteria provided in the text.

Then, get in touch with each person identified to enlist their help: You can either send a quick e-mail—that one-sentence explanation of your career aspirations will come in handy now—or make a brief phone call to explain what you're looking for. It's worth explaining why you chose them (e.g., "I know that your work brings you into contact with people from many different fields, and I thought you might know someone who works in _____.")

Friends Who Have Professional Dealings in Your Field

Name	Contact info	Potential contacts they know

The Network You Never Knew You Had (cont'd)

Highly Social Friends

Name	Contact info	Potential contacts they know
_____	_____	_____
_____	_____	_____
_____	_____	_____
_____	_____	_____
_____	_____	_____

Resourceful Friends

Name	Contact info	Potential contacts they know
_____	_____	_____
_____	_____	_____
_____	_____	_____
_____	_____	_____

The Network You Never Knew You Had (cont'd)

Your Fan Base

Name	Contact info	Potential contacts they know
_____	_____	_____
_____	_____	_____
_____	_____	_____
_____	_____	_____
_____	_____	_____

First Steps

Prepare Your Approach

Now you have your list of promising contacts—so you're ready to start calling people, right? Well, almost. First you'll want to have an introduction prepared. There are three ways to accomplish this: an e-mail, a call sheet, and a formal introductory letter.

E-Mail

Keep introductory e-mails short and to the point, but also personable—especially if you have friends in common. Mention your mutual friend's name right up front, if there is one, and explain your career crossroads as succinctly as possible. Explain why you think your contact might have some insight to offer. Throwing in a compliment about the person's reputation at this point couldn't hurt, as long as you don't lay it on too thick. Then wrap it up with an invitation to lunch or coffee, and suggest several days in the next couple of weeks that look good to you.

Here's an example:

Hi Bob—

My name is Jason Gargungle, and your cousin Samantha Silvers recommended that I contact you as someone who knows the Formula One racing scene inside and out. Running my own auto body shop has been rewarding these past 15 years, but it doesn't exactly satisfy my need for speed—and as an avid Formula One fan, being a racecar mechanic seems like the ultimate challenge. And who better to ask for the lowdown on what it's like to work the pits than the man Car and Driver *named "Mr. Quick Change" in the May issue?*

So I wonder if I could take just a few minutes of your time over coffee to hear a bit about where you see the field headed and any recommendations you might have for a relative novice. My time is flexible at the shop this month, so any time of day or evening Wednesday through Saturday in the next couple of weeks would be ideal. If there's another time that's more convenient for you, just let me know—I'm sure I can find a way to make it work. (That's our job, right?)

Samantha sends her best, to which I add my own.

—Jason Gargungle

[e-mail address]
[phone number]
[mailing address]

Use the workbook provided to prepare your own introductory e-mail.

The Approach: Writing Your E-Mail Intro

Writing your e-mail introduction isn't that hard if you break it into smaller pieces first.

Greeting: _____

_____

Introduction and mention of common friend/contact: _____

_____

Expression of interest/expertise in field (hint: use the sentence you worked out in the beginning of this chapter): _____

_____

_____

Reason contact was chosen: _____

_____

Reason for e-mail/invitation to lunch: _____

_____

_____

Scheduling suggestion: _____

_____

Closing: _____

Salutation: _____

Your contact info: _____

Phone Call

The phone call is a lot like the introductory e-mail, in that you'll need to keep it short, to the point, and as friendly as possible. Before you make any phone calls, you should prepare a call sheet, which should include the following:

1. Contact's name and preferably direct contact number. Be prepared to go through several assistants if the person has an important position or works in a big bureaucracy.

2. Introduction. Mention your mutual friend's name right up front, if you have one, and introduce yourself very quickly—you'll probably have less than 20 seconds before your contact gets impatient. Use the one-sentence descriptor you created at the beginning of this chapter—that's what it's for!

3. An explanation of why you are contacting this person. Write out your main points so you don't forget anything in the excitement of getting your contact on the other end of the phone. Be sure to explain why you think this person's insights would be valuable in your career research, and add a thoughtful compliment about the person's reputation before your contact has a chance to say no.

4. Pause, to give your contact a chance to respond. If your contact starts to launch into a full-fledged lecture about the field, you should be prepared to go with it. Once you've chatted awhile (but before the conversation starts to lose steam), you can segue into your invite. If your contact shows minimal interest, though, don't prolong the conversation with idle chatter—cut to the chase.

5. The invitation. You want to shift gears gradually and move directly into scheduling, so that there is no opportunity for the word "no" before you're finished: "You know, this is really fascinating, and I wonder if we might be

able to pick up this conversation over lunch sometime? I'm free next week on Tuesday and Wednesday, and anytime Wednesday through Friday the following week looks good, too. Is there any day you're free then, or some other time?"

6. Follow-up and conclusion. If your contact accepts your invitation, express your gratitude, set a date, mention you're looking forward to it, and sign off. If your contact says no, ask whether another time would be better or if he or she might be willing to refer you to someone else who might have valuable insights to share on the subject. If the answer is no, thank the person for his or her time, say goodbye, and move on.

Use the workbook provided to prepare your call sheet.

The Approach: Preparing Your Call Sheet

Refer to the guidelines in the text when filling in the blanks provided below to prepare for your introductory phone call.

Contact's name and phone number: _____

_____

Introduction: _____

_____

_____

_____

Reason for your phone call: _____

_____

_____

Invitation to lunch or coffee: _____

_____

_____

Follow-up and conclusion:

(when the answer is "yes") _____

_____

(when the answer is "no") _____

_____

_____

First Steps

Letters

Many people claim that writing a letter is the least effective way to establish contact, because there is a very real risk of your letter getting lost in someone's inbox and excessive politeness tends to establish a supplicant-authority hierarchy between you and your contact. But formal letters may be the more polite way to approach people who are much older and distinguished, and they are prevalent in geographic regions where formalities are more a part of the cultural and linguistic structures—the American South or Italy, for example.

If you can persuade a mutual friend, colleague, or notable person in your field to write a letter of introduction for you, so much the better. This provides you with an introduction and establishes your credentials in one fell swoop. If you are networking in a culture where your command of formal language is less than perfect, a letter of introduction in the lingua franca will help pave the way to a gracious welcome.

If you're writing the letter yourself, use the formal approach you were taught in school. If you get stuck, Microsoft Word (and most other word-processing software) features a letter-writing wizard that pops up as soon as you write the words "Dear Dr./Ms./Mr." to offer tips and a formal letter template. When you're done, you should have a letter of that looks like the sample approach letter on the next page.

Sample Approach Letter

[Date]
[Addressee name and title]
[Street address]

Dear Ms. Callahan,

My name is Tabitha Simmons, and your former employee James Wentworth recommended that I contact you in anticipation of my relocation to Dublin. It has been my considerable pleasure to work alongside James in the Technical Support division of ABC Software, Inc., in my capacity as Technical Support Manager. While I have found this to be a most rewarding position that has allowed me to acquire advanced client management and technical skills, my husband and I have recently made the decision to relocate to our native Dublin. Since I have much to learn about the tech industry in Ireland, James very kindly recommended that I speak to you as an expert on the subject.

I read your comments about the future of technology in Ireland in the October 30 issue of *The Independent* with great interest, and I was particularly intrigued by your comments regarding outsourcing of tech support by major Irish tech companies. Like many of its competitors in the United States, ABC Software, Inc., outsources many of its tech support operations overseas, so the team I managed was multinational in scope. The occasional 3 a.m. phone call notwithstanding, I found the multinational perspective of our team to be a real asset on both a business and personal level. As a result, I couldn't agree more with your conclusions that multinational teams give companies an edge in the global marketplace, and individual team members an edge in the increasingly global job market.

I would be honored and delighted if you could spare some time in your busy schedule to share further insights on the subject of technology and globalization trends in Ireland. I plan to be settled in Dublin by the end of December, and I hope we can schedule time for lunch or coffee early in the new year. I'll call you upon arrival, in the hopes that we might find a time that would be convenient for you.

Meanwhile, please accept best wishes from myself and James for a very happy holiday and a prosperous new year.

Kind regards,

Tabitha Sorenstam

Make the Approach

First Steps

You have prepared your list of contacts, introduction, and invitation, and you're finally ready to approach your contacts and set up some meetings. Bravo! Now it's time to take action, following the steps below:

1. **Prioritize.** Pick out the ten people from your list of contacts whom you think are most likely to have some knowledge of or dealings within your field of interest. Then identify a second, third, and fourth tier of candidates following the same criterion.

2. **Make initial contact.** Send e-mails or letters or place phone calls to the most promising contacts. Write an e-mail or letter (using the templates provided in the previous section) to each of these top ten contacts, or prepare a call sheet (using the template from the previous section) for each and make your phone calls. Keep track of the dates on which you contact each person.

3. **Follow up.** Pursue the most promising responses to your request first, and then work your way through them all. It's better to strike while the iron's hot, so be sure to acknowledge and follow up with any positive replies very soon after your personal contact has responded or has given you a referral—no more than a couple of days after you receive a response. See the next chapter for tips on scheduling your lunch.

   If someone sends you an e-mail to say that they don't know that much about the field or don't have time for lunch, send a response asking whether they would be willing to refer you to anyone they know who is knowledgeable about your interests. This process may yield plenty of

contacts and referrals to invite to lunch or coffee—both personal contacts who agree to meet you and people they refer you to.

For those who don't respond to your initial approach within a couple of weeks, you should attempt to make contact again. If you receive no response to your second query within a month, you can try one more time, this time asking whether they know of anyone they could refer you to. If you get a negative response, take it in stride, thank your contact for getting back to you, and move on.

4. **Lather, rinse, repeat.** Once you've followed up with everyone from tier 1, it's time to repeat the process for each additional tier of candidates.

5. **Solicit additional contacts.** After you've gone through your rounds of invites, send out a mass e-mail to others on your personal contacts list whom you don't think are particularly likely to have dealings with people in your chosen field. In this e-mail, simply ask them whether they know anyone who may be willing to talk to you about the subject. You may get a terrific response to this e-mail. Again, concentrate on the best responses first, and then work your way to the end of the list.

How to Handle Referrals

> It is far more impressive when others discover
> your good qualities without your help.
> —*Miss Manners (a.k.a. Judith Martin)*

Referrals are a special category of contact, so your process of contacting a referral will be slightly different. Follow these steps for contacting people who have been referred to you by members of your network.

Get Contact Information

If your mutual friend wants to check with the contact first to be sure it's alright to give out the contact's information, be understanding—and check in after a few days if you don't hear back right away. In addition to finding out a name and profession, you'll want to know a little about the contact's background and his or her exposure to the field you're interested in.

Request an Introduction

Find out whether the referrer is willing to make introductions on your behalf. This is the best way to guarantee a response from the contact, since the contact will feel obliged to the referrer to follow through. Explain to the referrer why you want to be in touch with the contact, and then ask whether he or she is willing to introduce you in person or via e-mail. Offer to provide a brief description of your background and interests (three or four sentences) that the

referrer can use in an introductory e-mail, to save the referrer's time and effort and to ensure that the right information is conveyed.

If your contact seems uncomfortable making the introduction, be understanding and ask, "Can I mention that you referred me?" Mentioning a mutual acquaintance in your initial approach will significantly increase your chance of a positive response, since your mutual friend may alert your contact to expect your call or e-mail and might follow up to find out how the conversation between you went.

Research

After you've gotten as much information about the contact as you can from the referrer, run a Google search on the contact's name to see what you can find out about his or her interests, background, and accomplishments. This information will provide essential background for an appropriate and winsome interaction and an effective introductory e-mail, phone call, or letter if you're not being introduced.

Making Connections
with Ease

- What to Expect

- Schedule Smart

- Prepare for Your Meeting

- Make Small Talk with Big Promise

- Follow Up

What to Expect

> The meeting of two personalities is like the contact of two chemical
> substances; if there is any reaction, both are transformed.
>
> —*Carl Jung*

Newsflash: There's no such thing as an "informational interview." A lunch or coffee meeting is not an interview. It's much more fun than that—and more important to your career. Lunch and coffee are casual scenarios, where you and your contact are free to explore personal connections, hobbies, mutual friends, and interests—not at all like an interview in an office setting, which is strictly business, never personal. Interviews usually entail answering a barrage of trick questions about your qualifications from multiple people under fluorescent lighting in highly constricting clothing—and if you succeed, you get to do it again another day with a whole new set of people. If that doesn't sound enticing to you, consider the alternative: meeting someone you have cause to admire in a comfortable setting to talk about dreams and aspirations, with the possibility of dessert thrown in for good measure.

And consider this: A good job interview might land you one job, of course, but a terrific lunch conversation could be the start of a relationship that may open up dozens of opportunities over the course of your career.

We've established that you needn't treat your lunch meeting like a formal job interview. But that doesn't mean you shouldn't take a few steps to ensure it goes off without a hitch.

Schedule Smart

To avoid playing phone tag and rescheduling, you should be prepared to suggest a good time and place to meet your contact. You know your schedule, so offer a few options that work for you. Be flexible, but don't say you're available "anytime"—you don't want to give your contact the impression that your time is so disposable that you can be put off for months or an appointment can be rescheduled ad infinitum. When it comes to selecting a place, we've provided some pointers to help you find appropriate venues.

Where to Meet: The Good and the Bad

Good venues for first contacts include:

- **A café.** Selecting a café suggests that this will be a casual encounter and gives you both the option of either cutting it short if you're in a hurry or lingering over your coffee if you really hit it off. Ask your contact to suggest a favorite café, or suggest a café conveniently located near your contact's workplace.

- **A restaurant with a good lunch menu and reliable service.** Waiting often brings out the worst in people—particularly hungry people. So pick a place where you know you can get a table quickly, expect prompt service, and get the check before the soporific post-lunch effect kicks in and conversation begins to stall. Again, be sure this restaurant is conveniently located for your contact.

- **Common ground.** If you know you're both headed to brunch at a mutual friend's place, the same local art opening, or film festival fundraiser, you could plan to meet there—or better yet, offer your contact a lift to the event as an added incentive to attend. Or if you know you share an interest with your contact—a particular author, say—you might suggest meeting at a bookstore for a reading by that author and going out for coffee afterward. Meeting on common ground makes it easy to make conversation and find points of connection.

81

Making Connections

On the other hand, bad ideas for initial points of contact would include:

- **A bar.** Unless your dining partner suggests it or is someone you know well—you don't want to give the impression that you're a lush or that this is a date.

- **The office.** Whether it's yours or theirs, the formal and distracting setting of an office makes for a less than congenial environment—not to mention countless interruptions.

- **A steakhouse or burger joint.** Unless you've already ascertained that your dining partner is not a vegetarian and likes nothing better than a juicy hunk of meat.

- **An ultra-swanky restaurant.** Lavish wining and dining can make it seem like you're trying too hard and make your contact suspicious of your motives. It can be a distraction, too: You want your dining partner to remember you, not the five-star menu. Formal settings can also make many people self-conscious, and you don't want your dining partner fretting over which utensil to use when you're trying to put that person at ease.

- **Your place.** Even if your offer to come up and check out your etchings is completely innocent, it might not be taken that way—and nothing makes a situation more awkward than perceived unwanted advances, on your end or theirs.

Reminders

Send a brief, gentle reminder e-mail the day before your meeting to confirm that you're still on for lunch or coffee. If you don't have an e-mail address, call the receptionist at your contact's workplace and ask to be transferred to your contact's voice mail so you can leave a message without interrupting his or her day.

Try an e-mail or voice mail message along these lines:

"Hi, [contact's first name]. This is [your first and last name]. I just wanted to let you know that I'm looking forward to meeting you in person tomorrow. If anything comes up, please let me know by calling my cell at [number]. Otherwise, I'll see you at [venue] at [time]."

Prepare for Your Meeting

Relax, already! There's no need to spend hours preparing for lunch or coffee as you would for a formal interview where you'd be interrogated about your credentials and intentions. That said, a few minor preparations might put your mind at ease so you can better relax, be yourself, and enjoy the food and the company.

The Week Before

Get geared up. Make sure your resume is updated, your work samples are in order, and you have a business card to hand out. If your favorite business-casual outfit needs dry-cleaning, do it now. If you're profoundly dissatisfied with your wardrobe options, now's the time to get one new item that will give you an extra boost of confidence. But there's no need to break the bank on an entire new outfit—it's only lunch!

The Day Before

Get everything in order. Send out your reminder to your contact. Make sure you have enough cash to cover lunch for two, in case credit cards aren't accepted or the machine is down. Lay out your outfit, making sure your shoes are polished and your clothes are spotless and wrinkle-free. Set aside any accessories you plan to wear, too—you don't want to tear through your drawers looking for a belt tomorrow. Pack up your bag or briefcase, including your wallet, keys, business cards, notebook, pen, a comb, and Band-Aids in case your good shoes give you blisters. It couldn't hurt to bring along a fresh copy of your resume, and you might want to bring along a couple of work samples just in case.

Then go to bed early to get a full night's sleep—nothing less than 8 hours will do.

The Day Of

Get up and treat yourself to a leisurely breakfast. Get to work a little early in case lunch runs a long. Take it easy with work—try to avoid anything that will raise your stress level. Then arrive at your venue ten minutes early, and wait patiently for your contact to arrive. Do not call your contact to confirm arrival until he or she is at least 15 minutes late, and express understanding when offered apologies for lateness—being gracious about tardiness will help put you in your contact's good graces. Then, have a good time—and be sure you pick up the check!

Make Small Talk with Big Promise

*He that knows how to make those he converses with easy, without debasing
himself to low and servile Flattery, has found the true Art of living
in the World, and being both welcome and valued everywhere.*

—John Locke

There's nothing small about small talk you make over lunch and coffee with a
contact—so while you want to be yourself, you should be on your best
behavior. Don't dominate the conversation. Ask questions, and look for
attributes you can appreciate or perhaps learn from in your contact. This
doesn't mean you should spend more time buttering up your contact than your
bread—but if you know your contact has done something you admire, bring it
up, and if your contact says something that strikes you as particularly astute,
point it out and explain why you think it's right. If you can't find actions or
statement that you connect to, you might find other attributes in your contact
that provide a point of connection. Does your contact share your taste in candy
or have a sense of humor that reminds you of your sister? You never know
what common bond will be the beginning of a satisfying working relationship,
or even a friendship. And never, ever miss an opportunity to offer a tip,
reference, or other help wherever you can—what comes around, goes around.

First Impressions

Even before you say a word, your body language is speaking volumes. Stand when your contact comes in, make eye contact, and smile as you say hello—it'll help break the ice. A nice firm handshake is a must, and if it's a colleague or acquaintance you're meeting, you might want to go with a warm, two-handed handshake. Close friends and relatives are the only contacts you can get away with hugging in this scenario, and even then you may want to make it a quick, one-armed hug to signal that you're here in an official capacity. The very first thing out of your mouth after your greeting should always be, "I really appreciate your willingness to meet me today."

Conversation Starters—and Nonstarters

You've invited your contact to lunch or coffee in part because you feel this person may have insights to share. Now's the time to get your contact talking and tap into that insight with some specific, open-ended questions—though be sure to wait until he or she is between bites, since most people don't like to talk with their mouths full.

Here are a few questions to get you started:

- What initially got you interested in your line of work?
- What's the strangest career change you've ever made?
- It's pretty bold to make a career change like yours. How did you pull that off?
- What's the best piece of advice you ever received about working in this field?
- How did you land your first job in the field?
- What is a typical workday for you?
- What is the most satisfying job you've ever had?
- Are there any books you'd particularly recommend on the subject?

- When you call a reference to check out a job candidate, what are you listening for?

- Do you know of any companies in this field that are hiring?

- Do you have any recommendations for someone just starting out?

- Is there something you do outside work that you find inspires you in your job?

- Do you ever think of going into business for yourself/going back to the corporate world? Why or why not?

- Is there a particular professional association, online discussion forum, website, or group you'd recommend I check out?

If your contact is coming up with a lot of great ideas, say, "This is terrific—I really should be getting some of this down. Would it bother you if I jotted down a few quick notes?" Almost everyone allows it—who doesn't like to think of her words as immortal? Then you can pull out a notebook and write a few keywords to jog your memory as your contact speaks. But don't lose eye contact entirely—be sure your focus is on your contact, not your notes. Your personal connection to your contact will be far more valuable to you than any notes.

At the end of the conversation, leave the door open for further discussion with a question along these lines: "Would you mind if I ask you some more questions about the field sometime, as I learn more about it?"

Whatever you do, avoid these three conversation nonstarters:

Prying. Contacts may not be able to fill you in on every detail of a project or company due to confidentiality clauses and personal loyalties, and they probably won't want to dish the dirt on coworkers with someone they don't know that well. So don't press the issue if someone diplomatically says, "He wasn't my favorite boss ever, but he never held me back and always made sure I had all the staff resources I needed to implement my new product ideas." You might pause here and give your contact a quizzical look to encourage further divulging, but don't say something like, "Oh yeah? What didn't you like about him, exactly?"

You don't want to come off as a gossip-monger. Also, don't ask questions about the organization's financials, lest your contact think you're a corporate spy of some kind—after all, everything you need to know you should be able to find in the annual report as a matter of public record. And by no means should you ever ask how much your contact earns—next to sexual habits, salaries are the most private information. Look up a salary survey in your chosen field if you want to know how much you can reasonably expect to make.

Bragging. There's a fine line between telling an anecdote about a project you tackled successfully to give your contact a sense of what you're capable of and bragging. If you find yourself telling more than three of these stories, listing awards you've received, or heaven forfend, honors you received in high school, you've crossed that line. Be humble: You're here to learn everything you can about your field from your contact, not to use this as an occasion to grandstand. There is such a thing as being too modest, though—don't brush off your accomplishment managing a million-dollar ad campaign as "no big deal."

Begging. Your contact has already done you the favor of meeting you for lunch to offer you career insights. Don't push your luck by begging for a referral, an interview, or a job. This calls your true motives for lunch into question, and your contact won't be pleased to feel duped or manipulated into meeting you. The odds of winning a job you beg for are very slim, and the odds of you winning anyone's respect (including your own) are even slimmer—which means that after this initial contact, your contact will probably cut you off. Earn your contact's respect instead of pity, and that contact may be willing to go to bat for you when hiring time comes around.

Opening Up

If your contact asks you questions, answer as openly, honestly, and thoughtfully as you can. If you're caught off guard with a tough question, pause and say, "You know, that's a really good question. Let me think about that. . . ." Then if you need more time, repeat the question. By then you've bought yourself 20 seconds of thinking time, so you should be able to come up with some response. If not, say, "That merits some serious thought. Can I get back to you on that one?" If you feel that a question is not something you can answer for reasons of confidentiality or loyalty, just say, "I'm not sure I can tell you about that one, because it was told to me in confidence. All I can say is what you probably already know of the situation, which is [publicly known fact]."

Anecdotally Speaking

You want to be sure that you leave a good impression of your professional capabilities, which means you should be prepared to tell a couple of stories about how you found an effective, creative solution to a problem your contact might appreciate. Keep it short, and make sure you ask a question or two to keep your contact engaged with what you're saying.

For example:

"Jose tells me you've created a really impressive intranet at your company. Those things can be tough to develop, can't they? But the results are definitely worth the trouble to get it right. I've never created a whole one from front to back myself, but I did create our company's benefits page. The deal was, our company had a great employee benefit program, but the old brochure explaining the details was so confusing that employees actually complained the company was being stingy with benefits. So as IT manager, I worked with the head of HR to come up with a benefits section on the intranet that highlighted all of the benefits available to employees and allowed them to sign up online. Now HR reports that not only employees have stopped

Making Connections

complaining about their benefits, they actually brag about the company benefits to people who come in to interview."

Dealing with Insider Jargon

If you don't understand the terminology or recognize the names your contact is tossing out, ask for clarification. There's nothing more embarrassing than pretending you know what someone is talking about and getting found out. If a name, word, or acronym that you're not familiar with comes up and it seems important, take out a notebook and pen and say, "Wait, I want to be sure I get this all down. How do you spell that, exactly?" Nobody knows all the people or jargon in the world—if you did know, you probably wouldn't need to be having lunch with all these people!

Minding Your Ps and Qs

Your grandmother wasn't leading you astray when she told you that people often appreciate good manners and always notice bad ones. To keep your grandmother happy, we've compiled a list of a few dos and don'ts:

Do let your dining partner order first, and follow your partner's lead when it comes to ordering dessert or post-lunch coffee. You don't want to keep your dining partner waiting while you finish your meal.

Do let your waiter know with a hand signal that you'll be the one picking up the check. Under no circumstances should you let your contact pick up the check, since your contact is doing you a favor by meeting with you. If you really hit it off and your contact is insisting on paying his or her share, offer to let your contact pick up the tab the next time you go out for coffee. This is a nice way to send a signal that this first meeting could be the beginning of a friendship.

Do remain respectful and appreciative of your dining partner's time. If your contact told you he or she could only get away for a quick lunch, be sure to say after a half an hour, "As much as I'd be delighted to continue this conversation, I don't want to keep you much longer if you have someplace you need to be." Your lunch partner may grant you a time extension at this point or agree that it's time to go. If he or she makes apologies about having to leave, restate how grateful you are for the time.

Don't be rude to the wait staff. Most people know better than to show up late for a first meeting—but according to a 2003 survey initiated by The Creative Group, the majority of 250 respondents considered lateness a less damaging gaffe than "being rude to wait staff," the number one lunch meeting mistake.[1] It makes you look like Dr. Jekyll and Mr. Hyde to be attentive and fawning to your contact one minute and harsh to your server the next.

Don't order something that is likely to take up visible residence in your teeth—like a poppy-seed bagel. Likewise, skip anything that will be messy or otherwise distracting.

Don't forget your table manners. Chew with your mouth closed, wait to swallow your food before you respond to a question, avoid slurping or smacking your lips, don't tilt your chair back like a kindergartner, and try not to wriggle or slump in your chair. You want your contact to remember you by your finer qualities, not your bizarre eating habits.

[1] The Creative Group press release. March 12, 2003.

Making Connections

Making Jokes without Being One

At the risk of stating the obvious, here goes: When you're trying to make an impression as a capable professional, it's probably not the most opportune time for self-deprecating jokes. In fact, you'll want to follow any quips you make with thoughtful insights to show you're not just a joker who can't take anything seriously. It's also better not to wisecrack at anyone's expense, even your contact's competitors. Snide remarks and one-upmanship reveal an unattractive mean streak that will make your contact wary of vouching for you and introducing you to others. You never know where your contacts used to work or consult or where their family and friends work.

Getting Propositioned, and Other Awkward Scenarios

If your contact suggests anything untoward, here's a no-fail out clause: "As flattered as I am at the offer, I'm going to have to say no." On the off chance your contact presses or entreats you, just say, "Thanks, but I can't." You don't need to give a reason or come up with an excuse—a good firm "no" needs no embellishment.

If the proposition your partner makes is financial in nature, just say, "Thanks, but I make all my investment plans/charitable contributions jointly with my family. If you have some materials on hand, I'd be happy to bring them home with me." You can use a similar line with someone trying to win you over to their political or religious perspectives: "I tend to disagree, but of course I value your viewpoint and will give it some thought. If you can think of a resource on the subject you think is especially valuable, I'd like to check that out."

Knowing When to Quit

Always quit while you're ahead. If things aren't going well despite your best efforts, ask for the check as soon as you're both finished and try to end on a bright note. Recap something you learned from the conversation, and thank your contact for taking the time to meet you and offer his or her useful insights. On the other hand, if you're lingering over the check because you're both enjoying the conversation, here's how to wrap things up: "I'm really enjoying our talk, but I'm mindful of your time. Maybe we could pick this up at a later date?"

It Could Happen to You: Is This a Date?

Sometimes you may feel such a connection to your contact that you begin to wonder whether your lunch date has turned into a *date* date. Don't let yourself get too carried away in the moment. Remember you're here in a professional capacity, and just as you would not smooch your boss in public (we hope) you should not smooch someone in public who could be your boss if he or she decides to pull a few strings on your behalf. No rumors are as pernicious as the ones about people who slept their way to the top.

How do you handle it when your contact asks you out on a date after your first meeting? If you really want to accept, there's nothing stopping you—but know that it may mean dropping your professional pursuits with this person. Again, you don't want your motives to be suspect.

If you're not interested, you need to find a diplomatic way to make that known without sacrificing the relationship. When one technology journalist was asked out to dinner by an editor, she shifted the relationship to a professional footing by saying, "Oh, I'm sorry, I don't really have any new story ideas to pitch just now, and I wouldn't want to waste your time.

But I'll get back to you as soon as I come up with some bright ideas I think are worthy of your magazine, and maybe we can plan to have coffee then." The editor took the hint.

Follow Up

Thorough follow-up entails six steps:

1. **Give thanks.** Send a nice thank-you note to your contact the day after your meeting, being sure to reference some specific, personal detail from the conversation.

2. **Pursue leads.** If your contact promised to send you a job lead, refer you to someone, or forward your resume, express your appreciation in advance as a gentle reminder to your contact to follow through. If you don't hear from the contact for a week or two after your card would have been received, you may need to send a follow-up reminder.

3. **Build a relationship.** Don't let the follow-up stop there—one lunch plus a quick note or two does not add up to a relationship. Keep your contact apprised of your career moves. Also keep an eye out for events, news items, and books that you think might interest your contact based on your conversation, and forward this information with a friendly note. Include your contact in your holiday card list, too.

4. **Extend invitations.** If you're headed to an event your contact might enjoy, you could invite him or her to meet you there and go for coffee afterward. If you host a big barbecue or holiday shindig every year, you could add your contact to the list if you hit it off and felt so inclined.

5. **Let yourself be mentored graciously.** Don't be insulted if your contact recommends that you read basic books on your field that are well below your skill level or tells you that you should try for an entry-level position.

Making Connections

Thank the contact kindly for the advice, and gently mention you've covered that area and now feel ready to take on some more challenging reading/roles. Is there anything along those lines he or she might suggest?

6. **Return the favor.** If ever you're in a position to be of help to your contact in any way—a recommendation of where to find vegetarian food in Dusseldorf, a quickie lesson in Photoshop, an introduction to a friend of yours who also started an ecotourism venture—offer it without hesitation and follow through on your promise. You could start a cycle of professional reciprocity that never ends (see "It Could Happen to You: Got Your Back").

 It Could Happen to You: Got Your Back

One entrepreneur got her first serious job interview out of college through a college friend who worked at the organization and recommended her personally and professionally. The friend moved to Europe shortly thereafter, but returned after a few years for grad school in need of a flexible interim job. She soon landed an ideal interim job working alongside—guess who?—her college buddy, who tipped her off about a colleague going on maternity leave in a position that the returned expatriate was ideally qualified to fill. They both went on to become independent entrepreneurs, but the mutual personal and professional admiration remains, and they often recommend one another to clients. Over the years, these mutual recommendations have helped each of them in their businesses.

One Step Ahead: Have You Thanked Your Contact Enough?

If a referral or interview the contact sets up leads to a job offer, be sure to send along a nice box of chocolates or a basket of some other gourmet treat you remember the contact liking. This isn't expected, of course—which is what makes it an unexpected pleasure. Add a note thanking that person for the referral, and mention that you'd welcome any opportunity to return the favor. When you have a triumph at a job your contact helped you land, write a note to let that contact know how well it's going, and how appreciative you still are for the help. Everyone likes to feel appreciated—and it's added incentive for kind gestures in the future.

Sometimes our light goes out but is blown again into flame by an encounter with another human being. Each of us owes the deepest thanks to those who have rekindled this inner light.

—attributed to Albert Schweitzer

The Next Level:
Advanced Networking

- Don't Stop Now

- Go Beyond Hero Worship

- Make a Change for the Better

- Strike Out on Your Own

Don't Stop Now

In a tough economy, where no job is secure and no person is impervious to stiff competition, "keeping your options open" may be synonymous with "keeping your contacts alive." So don't stop networking after you land a job—use this time to your advantage, to strengthen existing contacts and establish new ones.

Strengthen Your Existing Network

The first thing you should do when you land a job is to e-mail everyone you know with your new contact information and send personal thank-you notes and possibly small gifts to the references and contacts who helped you land the job. This is a nice way to show your appreciation, and it gives your contacts extra incentive to provide a reference or referral next time you're thinking of changing jobs. Even if it's been awhile since you've been in touch, there's no time like the present to reestablish contact. This also shows that you're not only interested in what your contact can do for you at a crucial juncture in your career, and that you intend to stay connected even when you don't need help with career advice. And whenever you leave a job, for whatever reason, send your new personal contact info to your office friends and co-workers you worked well with and take their information with you so you can stay in touch.

Here are some additional, easy ways you can strengthen your ties with your existing network:

1. **Become a credit to those who know you.** If you do good work and remain pleasant in your dealings with other people, you'll give your contacts the satisfaction of knowing they were wise in investing their time in you. And not incidentally, your exemplary performance and behavior help build your contact's reputation as someone who is a good judge of talent and character. All of this gives contacts added reason to vouch for your abilities and refer clients or employers to you.

2. **Make introductions.** The more friends and acquaintances you have in common with your contacts, the less likely they are to forget about you. So referring potential clients, employers, or ace employees to your contact is not only a nice way to return a favor—it's also a good way to reinforce your ties.

3. **Advice: Give as good as you get.** Pass along tips, interesting articles, or job postings that you have reason to believe may be of help to your contacts. This is good form and helps keep the lines of information in working order at times when you aren't particularly in need of advice. It also reminds your contacts that the relationship is beneficial to both parties.

Grow Your Network

Another immediate concern in any new job is establishing contacts within your new workplace. Whatever you do your first week on the job, don't work through lunch—take the opportunity to get to know your co-workers. You'll save yourself time and trouble by learning from those already in the know—who to approach in the IT department about computer trouble; the protocol on comp time, overtime, or working from home; when you're really expected to arrive in the office in the morning; and how to sidestep tricky office politics. Most important, you'll begin to recognize some friendly faces in the crowd that you can look forward to seeing every morning.

But as you seek out new contacts who might be able to help you manage your new responsibilities, don't let your efforts become entirely contained within the walls of your office. You want to keep your options open in your field, too, in case your current organization falls on hard times. So become a known presence in your field by:

- **Joining professional associations.** These give you an automatic connection to hundreds or possibly thousands of others in your field, and their advice can prove instrumental when it comes to negotiating a raise, taking on new responsibilities, handling layoffs, and starting a business.

- **Making yourself known.** Speeches, panels, and other public appearances will help raise your profile in your field, helping to build a fan base you can count on for support without having to seek them out individually.

- **Traveling for work.** Traveling gives you a chance to meet leading professionals in your field whom you might not otherwise encounter. Try to embrace opportunities to travel for work, and build some downtime into your schedule to allow you to meet with local professionals in your niche. Ask friends who live in the area you're visiting whether they have any recommendations.

- **Mentoring.** Every time you agree to lunch or coffee with someone trying to break into your field, you establish the foundation for a rewarding reciprocal relationship. Don't expect anything but lunch out of it, and you may be pleasantly surprised.

Maintain Your Contacts

Search through your inbox alphabetically by name, and if you come across any e-mails you owe a response to or find e-mails from people you haven't heard from in awhile, fire off a friendly e-mail as soon as possible. And with people you'd really enjoy seeing again, suggest coffee sometime in the near future to catch up.

It Could Happen to You: Sweeter than Candy

Like many of her peers during the dot-com boom, a woman we'll call Olivia left her comfy but somewhat lackluster management job for a fast-paced dot com. But unlike most of her peers, Olivia brought one piece of vital office equipment with her: her candy dish. At her new job, her desk was in a separate room from most of the rest of the company—but her tucked-away desk soon became a high-traffic area due to the dish she kept well-stocked with a variety of seasonal and often unusual candy. Everyone from overworked engineers to VPs and the CEO stopped by to sample what was new and chat—after all, it's rude to take candy without stopping to say hello, right? When the dot com folded a matter of months later, many of Olivia's co-workers fell out of touch. But Olivia had bonded with a number of her co-workers, and when she started her own business these people became her closest allies, steady clients, and most reliable vendors. Olivia estimates that over the years, she has earned more than $20,000 in contracts originating from former co-workers she met over that candy dish—and more important, she has the invaluable privilege of working alongside friends.

Go Beyond Hero Worship

If you're already plenty comfortable with networking and resilient enough not to be particularly bothered by nonresponsiveness, take it up a notch and try approaching people you particularly admire. To pull this off, you'll need four things working for you:

1. **Contact information.** You may need to do some online research to come up with the right work address or work phone number, and this can take time.

2. **Friendliness.** To reach your personal hero, you may first have to convince an assistant to put you through or provide accurate contact info.

3. **Brevity.** You'll need to be able to introduce yourself succinctly and sum up your career crossroads in very few words. Paging your career aspirations in one sentence . . .

4. **Tenacity.** You'll need to know going in that at best you'll reach one in ten people by cold calling and sending blind e-mails—but if you can keep the faith and try until you get to that tenth person, it can really be worth your while (see "It Could Happen to You: Mighty Mentors").

It Could Happen to You: Mighty Mentors

One operations manager for a local TV station enjoyed his job, but troubling world events made him realize that he wanted to do more to prevent conflict in the world. So he asked a few people to recommend books on the subject, and over the course of a summer, he worked his way through 20 classic texts about conflict. He took notes as he read and did some research to find contact information on the authors. Then one by one, he cold-called the authors. His introduction included references to the book he'd read and mentioned how it had influenced his thinking about returning to school for a Ph.D. in anthropology to study conflict. Then he asked each if they could spare a few minutes to talk about programs in the field. The response was phenomenal: No one hung up on him, most gave him far more time than he'd asked for, and three ended up offering him recommendations for grad school—including one world-renowned authority who spoke to him for two and a half hours and has remained in contact with him. In part through the weight of that author's recommendations, our networking hero landed a scholarship worth tens of thousands of dollars and an assistant researcher position at one of the top five anthropology programs in the country.

Here's the networking map for this feat of fearless cold-calling:

5 friends' book recommendations ⟶ 20 authors
⟶ 3 recommendations ⟶ 1 big career change

The Next Level

Make a Change for the Better

If you're contemplating a career change, some advanced networking strategies can help you take the leap and make a soft landing:

1. **Go social.** If you've kept up your contacts, your first step to a successful career change is putting out feelers about your interests. When people ask what you're up to, just give them the one-sentence career crossroads speech you drafted earlier. You may want to choose your venues judiciously, though, if you don't want your boss to know you're thinking of leaving just yet.

2. **Volunteer.** This is a good way to see if your putative new career really is as satisfying for you as you've heard it might be from contacts—and to meet new contacts in the field. You might also come away with some excellent work samples to show for it and added confidence from successfully helping others with your skills. All in all, it's a small investment of your time that can offer multiple rewards—including the pure pleasure of helping others.

3. **Publish.** Seems like everyone has their own Web 'zine or blog these days, so why not you too? Writing a guest editorial for the paper or pitching a story to a trade magazine in your field can give you a big boost of visibility in your field and added credentials to boot.

4. **Join a class, even if you think you know it all.** Find out what's changed in the field since you went through your training, and get to know peers who can keep you inspired and on track to achieving your goals.

5. **Drop hints while employed—with care.** Some discretion may be necessary here, if your employer isn't aware of your intentions or you want to keep

your options open. On the other hand, your boss may be more understanding about your need to leave work on time if you're up front about the class you're taking—some employers even pay for tuition. Some employers may be more appreciative and accommodating if they know you have options elsewhere.

 It Could Happen to You: From Dabbler to Pro

One bright film-school major wound up in the back room of an ad agency, editing ads he found mindless and boring. So he decided to make a satirical silent film short from odds and ends of film that wound up on the cutting-room floor, spliced together with titles he invented. Word got around of his talent with titles through a DJ friend at the agency, and he was invited to do motion graphics for a couple of music videos for local bands. His inventive efforts brought him to the attention of the local arts scene, and soon he was being asked to do distinctive titles for documentary films and, eventually, television series and movies. He has since relocated to a swank home in Los Angeles, where he now runs a booming business and can afford to hire other people to do any mindless or boring editing work.

The Next Level

Strike Out on Your Own

There's a strong argument that the most essential career qualification for any entrepreneur is not capital at all, but rather a strong network. Think about it: As a new business, your first and often most loyal clients are likely to be contacts you have made over the years. These people have some history with you, hence more reason than most to believe you can deliver on your word. To be successful these days, a business also needs reliable, honest vendors; strong technical support; and a great accountant—and to fill this bill, you need recommendations you can trust. Your network can not only help set you up in business, but it may very well keep you in business through personal referrals and testimonials when times are tough and advertising returns are down. Capital is easy-come, easy-go, but a network will see you through good times and bad.

Entrepreneurs have to make special efforts to maintain strong networks, since these provide the foundation for their professional reputation. The following are five networking considerations entrepreneurs should be especially mindful of.

The Difference between Contacts and Clients

Clients already have an established interest in your products or services, so it's fine for you to discuss their relative merits or new offerings at length. With contacts who have established no such interest yet, this would be dull and rude—they might expect a sales pitch from a salesperson, but not from someone they know primarily as a friend of their cousin's or business-school pal of a co-worker. Explain what you do, by all means, but don't forget that this is a chance for you to get to know and learn from someone in your field.

Mind Your Ethics

Conflicts of interest can and will arise with contacts, and you have to use your best judgment in handling them. Is it kosher to drum up business for your firm from your fellow nonprofit board members while you're serving as chairman of that board? Are you sure the relatively inexperienced friend you're using as a subcontractor really merits the hourly rate the client is paying? Should you pay a finder's fee to a contact for initially putting you in touch with a new hire? It's an ethical quagmire out there, so you better know where you stand on these issues before you wade too far out.

Watch Out for Burning Bridges

One burned bridge with a contact can be damaging to an entrepreneur's reputation, even if the entrepreneur was quite right to sever the ties. While the spurned contact may decide to take any grievances public, the entrepreneur will probably only make matters worse by refuting the charges and prolonging the debate. But if a contact has demanded payback for a referral in unlimited free services, it may be worth the damage control involved to end the exploitative relationship.

Stay Top of Mind

Entrepreneurs need to know that not only will their contacts remember them, but they will remember them *first* when a need arises for their goods or services. This means making extra effort to be thoughtful, sending more personal notes, issuing more invitations to events, staying on top of the latest developments in the field, and generally being more social—all this, and somehow finding time to do stellar work on the job.

The Next Level

Share the Wealth

Entrepreneurs depend on their community for their very livelihood, so they need to foster it by donating funds to worthy organizations in their community and their field, imparting their knowledge to the next generation in their field, and occasionally providing services or goods to community-based organizations at low or no cost. This builds goodwill in the community, which returns to entrepreneurs tenfold with new contacts who have heard of their good works, clients whose loyalty is cemented through a shared concern for the community, universities who send the best graduates in their direction, and above all the daily satisfaction of living well and doing good at the same time.

And all people linve, not by reason of any care they have for themselves, but by the loves for them that is in other people.
—*attributed to Leo Tolstoy*

Online Resources

- Networking Sites

- Community Sites

- Sites for Creative Networking

- Career Research Sites

Networking Sites

LinkedIn (www.linkedin.com): A networking site for business professionals.

MeetUp (www.meetup.com): The 2003 Webby "Best Community Site" winner that organizes local interest groups ranging from Elvis Presley fans in Brisbane, Australia to stay-at-home moms in Raleigh, North Carolina.

Returned Peace Corps Volunteers Foundation (www.rpcv.org): Nonprofit foundation for returned Peace Corps Volunteers; a model to which other networking groups aspire.

Ryze (http://new.ryze.com/index.php): A networking site for business professionals that won a 2003 Forbes Favorite award; join and jump into the discussions or start your own interest group cluster.

Tribe.net (www.tribe.net): A newer entry to the ranks of social-networking sites, Tribe has been compared to Friendster, but described as less focused on dating.

Plus: Your school's alumni association website—there may even be a community forum just for the people who graduated in your year.

Your professional association's website.

Community Sites

AsianAvenue.com: community site for Asian Pacific Americans.

BlackPlanet.com: African American community forum.

Citysearch (www.citysearch.com): A community site to find people who share your interests and activity partners in your town.

Craigslist (www.craigslist.com): A community site to find people who share your interests and activity partners in your town; some regular users swear by this site for job leads and contacts.

Digital City (www.digitalcity.com): A community site to find people who share your interests and activity partners in your town.

MiGente.com (www.migente.com): Latino community site.

Thorn Tree (http://thorntree.lonelyplanet.com): Meeting place and resource center for world travelers.

Sites for Creative Networking

LiveJournal (http://www.livejournal.com): Webby-nominated blog site that allows you to publish your thoughts online, and strike up conversations with visitors who respond.

Blog-Spot (www.blogspot.com): Popular blogging site that gives you the chance to make your digital presence known, and others to respond to your ideas.

The Mail Art Project (http://nervousness.org/index.php): Start or add to an art project that gets mailed around the world—and meet and collaborate with people you never would have met otherwise.

Career Research Sites

CareerJournal (www.careerjournal.com): Wall Street Journal's special online section containing a repository of career-related articles, interviews about the outlooks of various professions, salary surveys, and more.

NaceWeb (www.naceweb.org): Provides statistical data on career prospects and trends for recent graduates.

U.S. Bureau of Labor Statistics' site (www.bls.gov): Provides labor market projections and other data on many fields.

WetFeet's site (www.wetfeet.com): Provides careers overviews and outlooks in many industries.

WetFeet's Insider Guide Series

Ace Your Case! The WetFeet Insider Guide to Consulting Interviews
Ace Your Case II: Fifteen More Consulting Cases
Ace Your Case III: Practice Makes Perfect
Ace Your Case IV: The Latest and Greatest
Ace Your Interview! The WetFeet Insider Guide to Interviewing
Beat the Street: The WetFeet Insider Guide to Investment Banking Interviews
Getting Your Ideal Internship
Get Your Foot in the Door! Landing the Job Interview
Job Hunting A to Z: The WetFeet Insider Guide to Landing the Job You Want
Killer Consulting Resumes!
Killer Cover Letters and Resumes!
Killer Investment Banking Resumes!
Negotiating Your Salary and Perks
Networking Works! The WetFeet Insider Guide to Networking

Career and Industry Guides

Accounting
Advertising and Public Relations
Asset Management and Retail Brokerage
Biotech and Pharmaceuticals
Brand Management
Health Care
Human Resources
Computer Software and Hardware
Consulting for Ph.D.s, Lawyers, and Doctors
Industries and Careers for MBAs
Industries and Careers for Undergrads
Information Technology
Investment Banking

Management Consulting
Manufacturing
Marketing and Market Research
Non-Profits and Government Agencies
Oil and Gas
Real Estate
Sports and Entertainment
Top 20 Biotechnology and Pharmaceutical Firms
Top 25 Consulting Firms
Top 25 Financial Services Firms
Top 20 Law Firms
Venture Capital

Company Guides

Accenture
Bain & Company
Bear Stearns
Booz Allen Hamilton
The Boston Consulting Group
Cap Gemini Ernst & Young
Citigroup's Corporate and Investment Bank
Credit Suisse First Boston
Deloitte Consulting
Goldman Sachs
IBM Business Consulting Services
JPMorgan Chase
Lehman Brothers
McKinsey & Company
Merrill Lynch
Monitor Group
Morgan Stanley